# AAT

## Personal Tax
## FA 2020

Level 4

Professional Diploma in Accounting

## Question Bank

For assessments from January to December 2021

Fifth edition 2020

ISBN 9781 5097 3504 4

**British Library Cataloguing-in-Publication Data**

A catalogue record for this book is available from the British Library

**Published by**

BPP Learning Media Ltd
BPP House, Aldine Place
142-144 Uxbridge Road
London W12 8AA

www.bpp.com/learningmedia ·

Printed in the United Kingdom

> Your learning materials, published by BPP Learning Media Ltd, are printed on paper obtained from traceable sustainable sources.

# Contents

# Introduction

This is BPP Learning Media's AAT Question Bank for *Personal Tax*. It is part of a suite of ground-breaking resources produced by BPP Learning Media for AAT assessments.

This Question Bank has been written in conjunction with the BPP Course Book, and has been carefully designed to enable students to practise all of the learning outcomes and assessment criteria for the units that make up *Personal Tax*. It is fully up to date as at August 2020 and reflects both the AAT's qualification specification and the practice assessment provided by the AAT.

This Question Bank contains tasks corresponding to each chapter of the Course Book. Some tasks are designed for learning purposes, others are of assessment standard.

The emphasis in all tasks and assessments is on the practical application of the skills acquired.

Assessments up to 31 December 2021 will use the rules contained in Finance Act 2020 so tasks will focus on tax rates and thresholds for the tax year 2020/21 and financial year 2020. It may be that you have to deal with other tax years at work, in which case the rates and thresholds you use will be different. This Question Bank is focused on your assessment up to 31 December 2021.

## VAT

You may find tasks throughout this Question Bank that need you to calculate or be aware of a rate of VAT. This is stated at 20% in these examples and questions.

## Approaching the assessment

When you sit the assessment, it is very important that you follow the on-screen instructions. This means you need to carefully read the instructions, both on the introduction screens and during specific tasks.

When you access the assessment, you should be presented with an introductory screen with information similar to that shown below.

We have provided this **sample assessment** to help you familiarise yourself with our e-assessment environment. It is designed to demonstrate as many of the question types that you may find in a live assessment as possible. It is not designed to be used on its own to determine whether you are ready for a live assessment.

You will receive a result for tasks 2, 3, 4, 5, 7, 8, 11 and 13 at the end of this assessment. Equivalents of tasks 1, 6, 10 and 13 will be human marked in the live assessment.

**Assessment information:**

You have **2 hours and 30 minutes** to complete this sample assessment.

This assessment contains **13 tasks** and you should attempt to complete every task.
Each task is independent. You will not need to refer to your answers in previous tasks.
Read every task carefully to make sure you understand what is required.

Task 1 requires extended writing as part of your response to the question. You should make sure you allow adequate time to complete this task.

Where the date is relevant, it is given in the task data.

You may use minus signs or brackets to indicate negative numbers **unless** task instructions say otherwise.

You must use a full stop to indicate a decimal point.
For example, write 100.57 NOT 100,57 or 100 57

You may use a comma to indicate a number in the thousands, but you don't have to.
For example, 10000 and 10,000 are both acceptable.

If rounding is required, normal mathematical rounding rules should be applied **unless** task instructions say otherwise.

The actual instructions will vary depending on the subject you are studying for. It is very important you read the instructions on the introductory screen and apply them in the assessment. You don't want to lose marks when you know the correct answer just because you have not entered it in the right format.

In general, the rules set out in the AAT practice assessments for the subject you are studying for will apply in the real assessment, but you should carefully read the information on this screen again in the real assessment, just to make sure.

A full stop is needed to indicate a decimal point. We would recommend using minus signs to indicate negative numbers and leaving out the comma signs to indicate thousands, as this results in a lower number of keystrokes and less margin for error when working under time pressure. Having said that, you can use whatever is easiest for you as long as you operate within the rules set out for your particular assessment.

You have to show competence throughout the assessment, and you should therefore complete all of the tasks. Don't leave questions unanswered.

Written or complex tasks will be human marked. In this case you are given a blank space or table to enter your answer into. You are told in the assessments which tasks these are.

When these involve calculations, it is a good idea to decide in advance how you are going to lay out your answers to such tasks by practising answering them on a word document, and certainly you should try all such tasks in this Question Bank and in the AAT's environment using the sample assessment.

When asked to fill in tables, or gaps, never leave any blank even if you are unsure of the answer. Fill in your best estimate.

Note that for some assessments where there is a lot of scenario information or tables of data provided (eg tax tables), you may need to access these via 'pop-ups'. Instructions will be provided on how you can bring up the necessary data during the assessment.

Finally, take note of any task specific instructions once you are in the assessment. For example, you may be asked to enter a date in a certain format or to enter a number to a certain number of decimal places.

## Grading

To achieve the qualification and to be awarded a grade, you must pass all the mandatory unit assessments, all optional unit assessments (where applicable) and the synoptic assessment.

The AAT Level 4 Professional Diploma in Accounting will be awarded a grade. This grade will be based on performance across the qualification. Unit assessments and synoptic assessments are not individually graded. These assessments are given a mark that is used in calculating the overall grade.

### How overall grade is determined

You will be awarded an overall qualification grade (Distinction, Merit, and Pass). If you do not achieve the qualification you will not receive a qualification certificate, and the grade will be shown as unclassified.

The marks of each assessment will be converted into a percentage mark and rounded up or down to the nearest whole number. This percentage mark is then weighted according to the weighting of the unit assessment or synoptic assessment within the qualification. The resulting weighted assessment percentages are combined to arrive at a percentage mark for the whole qualification.

| Grade definition | Percentage threshold |
|---|---|
| Distinction | 90 – 100% |
| Merit | 80 – 89% |
| Pass | 70 – 79% |
| Unclassified | 0 – 69%<br>Or failure to pass one or more assessments |

### Re-sits

**The AAT Professional Diploma In Accounting is not subject to re-sit restrictions.**

You should only be entered for an assessment when you are well-prepared and you expect to pass the assessment.

## AAT qualifications

The material in this book may support the following AAT qualifications:

AAT Professional Diploma in Accounting Level 4, AAT Professional Diploma in Accounting at SCQF Level 8.

## Supplements

From time to time we may need to publish supplementary materials to one of our titles. This can be for a variety of reasons. From a small change in the AAT unit guidance to new legislation coming into effect between editions.

You should check our supplements page regularly for anything that may affect your learning materials. All supplements are available free of charge on our supplements page on our website at:

www.bpp.com/learning-media/about/students

## Improving material and removing errors

There is a constant need to update and enhance our study materials in line with both regulatory changes and new insights into the assessments.

From our team of authors BPP appoints a subject expert to update and improve these materials for each new edition.

Their updated draft is subsequently technically checked by another author and from time to time non-technically checked by a proofreader.

We are very keen to remove as many numerical errors and narrative typos as we can but given the volume of detailed information being changed in a short space of time, we know that a few errors will sometimes get through our net.

We apologise in advance for any inconvenience that an error might cause. We continue to look for new ways to improve these study materials and would welcome your suggestions. If you have any comments about this book, the BPP author of this edition can be emailed at: learningmedia@bpp.com.

# Question Bank

# Chapter 1 – Taxable income

## Task 1.1

For each of the following sources of income, indicate whether it is non-savings income, savings income or dividend income by ticking the relevant box:

| | Non-savings income | Savings income | Dividend income |
|---|---|---|---|
| Trading income | ✓ | | |
| Dividend received from a company | | | |
| Property income | | | |
| Building society interest | | | |
| Bank interest | | | |
| Pension income | | | |
| Employment income | | | |
| Interest from government stock ('gilts') | | | |

## Task 1.2

Olive received the following income in 2020/21.

**Show the amount of income that she should enter on her tax return. If the income is exempt, enter 0.**

**(a)** Bank account interest £160

£ 

**(b)** Premium bond prize £100

£ 

**(c)** Dividends £540

£

## Task 1.3

**For each of the following interest payments, indicate whether they are received gross, net of tax or are exempt from income tax by ticking the relevant box:**

|  | Gross | Net | Exempt |
|---|---|---|---|
| Bank interest |  |  |  |
| Interest on an individual savings account (ISA) |  |  | ✓ |
| Employment income |  | ✓ |  |
| Interest from government stock ('gilts') | ✓ |  |  |

## Task 1.4

You act for Jonty. The following information is relevant for the year ended 5 April 2021:

(1)  His salary was £38,730.

(2)  His other income received was:

|  | £ |
|---|---|
| Building society interest | 80 |
| Dividends | 63 |

**Jonty's taxable income for 2020/21 is:**

£ 36,273

## Task 1.5

Mr Betteredge has the following income for 2020/21:

|  | £ |
|---|---|
| Salary for the year to 5 April 2021 | 15,665 |
| Interest received (amount received shown): |  |
| National Westminster Bank plc | 457 |
| ISA account | 180 |
| Nationwide Building Society account | 400 |

**Using the proforma layout provided, prepare a schedule of income for 2020/21, clearly showing the distinction between non-savings and savings income. If income is exempt, enter 0. Mr Betteredge's personal allowance should be deducted as appropriate. Fill in ALL the unshaded boxes and add a 0 (zero) if necessary.**

|  | Non-savings income £ | Savings income £ | Total £ |
|---|---|---|---|
| Earnings |  |  |  |
| Bank deposit interest |  |  |  |
| Building society interest |  |  |  |
| ISA interest |  |  |  |
| Net income |  |  |  |
| Less personal allowance |  |  |  |
| Taxable income |  |  |  |

## Task 1.6

Hayley receives employment income of £95,000, bank interest of £1,600, ISA interest of £2,000 and dividends of £4,500 in 2020/21.

(a) **Hayley's net income for 2020/21 is:**

£ [ ]

(b) **The personal allowance that Hayley is entitled to for 2020/21 is:**

£ [ ]

## Task 1.7

Max has net income of £116,000 for 2020/21. He made Gift Aid donations of £4,000 (gross) during the year.

**Max's personal allowance for 2020/21 is:**

£ [ ]

## Task 1.8

In 2020/21, Gavin receives pension income of £19,300, bank interest of £2,000, dividends of £5,400 and lottery winnings of £6,000.

**(a)** Gavin's net income for 2020/21 is:

£ _____

**(b)** The personal allowance that Gavin is entitled to for 2020/21 is:

£ _____

## Task 1.9

**From 6 April 2020 the maximum an individual can invest for the tax year in an ISA is:**

£ _____

## Task 1.10

**Tick to show whether the following statement is True or False.**

Scholarships and educational grants are exempt as income of the student.

|       | ✓ |
|-------|---|
| True  |   |
| False |   |

## Task 1.11

**Tick to show whether the following statement is True or False.**

Damages received for an injury at work are only sometimes exempt from income tax, whereas damages paid on death are always exempt from income tax.

|       | ✓ |
|-------|---|
| True  |   |
| False |   |

# Chapter 2 – Calculation of income tax

## Task 2.1

Guy receives bank interest of £7,500 in 2020/21.

**Calculate the income tax liability assuming he has non savings income before PA of:**

(a)   **£12,850 (show whole pounds only)**

£ 

(b)   **£51,850 (show whole pounds only)**

£ 

- - - - - - - - - - - - - - - - - - - - - - - - - - - - - - - - - - - - - - - - - - - - - - - - -

## Task 2.2

You act for Deidre Watkins. Deidre has the following taxable income for 2020/21:

Non-savings income      £14,700
Savings income          £2,176
Dividend income         £1,766

**Calculate Deidre's tax liability (show whole pounds only) on each source of income for 2020/21 as follows:**

(a)   **Non-savings income:**

£ 

(b)   **Savings income:**

£ 

(c)   **Dividend income:**

£ 

- - - - - - - - - - - - - - - - - - - - - - - - - - - - - - - - - - - - - - - - - - - - - - - - -

## Task 2.3

Peter has non-savings income of £205,000 and makes a personal pension contribution of £12,000 in December 2020.

**Tick to show the amount of Peter's additional rate threshold in 2020/21.**

|  | ✓ |
|---|---|
| £150,000 |  |
| £162,000 |  |
| £165,000 | ✓ |
| £153,000 |  |

## Task 2.4

Tony is a higher rate taxpayer and makes a Gift Aid donation of £6,000 in December 2020.

**Tick to show the amount of Tony's basic rate band in 2020/21.**

|  | ✓ |
|---|---|
| £43,500 |  |
| £37,500 |  |
| £45,000 | ✓ |
| £30,000 |  |

## Task 2.5

Katy is an additional rate taxpayer and makes a Gift Aid donation of £4,000 in June 2020.

**(a)** **Katy's basic rate band for 2020/21 is:**

£ [                ]

**(b)** **Katy's additional rate threshold for 2020/21 is:**

£ [                ]

**(c)** **Katy's higher rate band for 2020/21 is:**

£ [                ]

## Task 2.6

Ruth has non-savings income of £30,000, savings income of £2,000 and dividend income of £6,000.

**(a)** **Ruth's personal savings allowance for 2020/21 is:**

£ [                ]

**(b)** **Ruth's dividend allowance for 2020/21 is:**

£ [                ]

## Task 2.7

Rachel received £24,350 bank interest in 2020/21. This is her only income.

**Rachel's income tax liability for 2020/21 is:**

£ [                ]

## Task 2.8

Richard has taxable non-savings income of £58,525 in 2020/21. He made pension contributions to his personal pension scheme of £10,800 during the year. Tax of £9,700 was deducted under the PAYE system.

**Richard's income tax payable for 2020/21 is:**

| £ | |
|---|---|

## Task 2.9

John Smith has the following income and outgoings for the tax year 2020/21:

| | £ |
|---|---|
| Salary (£7,570 tax deducted under PAYE) | 50,850 |
| Interest on a deposit account with the Scotia Bank | 800 |
| Donation under the Gift Aid scheme made on 1 September 2020 | 2,400 |
| Dividends received on UK shares | 1,000 |

(a) **Using the proforma layout provided, prepare a schedule of income for 2020/21, clearly showing the distinction between non-savings, savings and dividend income. Fill in all the unshaded boxes. If an answer is zero input 0.**

| | Non-savings income £ | Savings income £ | Dividend income £ | Total £ |
|---|---|---|---|---|
| Salary | | | | |
| Dividend | | | | |
| Bank deposit interest | | | | |
| Net income | | | | |
| Less personal allowance | | | | |
| Taxable income | | | | |

**(b)** **John's income tax liability for 2020/21 is:**

£ [ ]

**(c)** **John's income tax payable for 2020/21 is:**

£ [ ]

..............................................................................

## Task 2.10

Jean Brown has the following income and outgoings for the tax year 2020/21:

|  | £ |
|---|---|
| Salary (£48,500 tax deducted under PAYE) | 155,000 |
| Interest on a bank deposit account | 3,000 |
| Personal pension contribution | 8,000 |
| Dividends received on UK shares | 10,000 |

**(a)** **Using the proforma layout provided, prepare a schedule of income for 2020/21, clearly showing the distinction between non-savings, savings and dividend income. Fill in all the unshaded boxes. If an answer is zero input 0.**

|  | Non-savings income £ | Savings income £ | Dividend income £ | Total £ |
|---|---|---|---|---|
| Salary |  |  |  |  |
| Dividend |  |  |  |  |
| Bank deposit interest |  |  |  |  |
| Net income |  |  |  |  |
| Less personal allowance |  |  |  |  |
| Taxable income |  |  |  |  |

**(b)** **Jean's income tax liability for 2020/21 is:**

£ [ ]

**(c)** **Jean's income tax payable for 2020/21 is:**

£ [ ]

..............................................................................

BPP
LEARNING MEDIA

11

## Task 2.11

**This style of task is human marked in the live assessment.**

During 2020/21 Joshua has income as follows:

| | |
|---|---|
| Pension income | £10,050 |
| Bank interest received | £11,075 |
| Dividends received | £10,000 |

Joshua made a Gift Aid donation of £1,500 in July 2020.

**Calculate Joshua's total income tax liability for 2020/21, using the table given below. Show your answer in whole pounds.**

| | | | | |
|---|---|---|---|---|
| | | | | |
| | | | | |
| | | | | |
| | | | | |
| | | | | |
| | | | | |
| | | | | |
| | | | | |
| | | | | |
| | | | | |
| | | | | |
| | | | | |
| | | | | |
| | | | | |
| | | | | |
| | | | | |
| | | | | |

## Task 2.12

**This style of task is human marked in the live assessment.**

During 2020/21 Jack has income as follows:

| | |
|---|---|
| Trading income | £90,000 |
| Bank interest received | £1,500 |
| Dividends received | £15,000 |

**Calculate Jack's total income tax liability for 2020/21, using the table given below. Show your answer in whole pounds.**

| | | | | £ |
|---|---|---|---|---|
| | | | | |
| | | | | |
| | | | | |
| | | | | |
| | | | | |
| | | | | |
| | | | | |
| | | | | |
| | | | | |
| | | | | |
| | | | | |
| | | | | |

# Chapter 3 – Employment income

## Task 3.1

**Show whether the following statement is True or False.**

An employee has a contract for services.

|  | ✓ |
|---|---|
| True | |
| False | |

........................................................................

## Task 3.2

Peter undertakes some work for XYZ plc.

**Tick which of the following factors would indicate that he either has a contract of service with XYZ plc or a contract for services.**

| Factor | Contract of service | Contract for services |
|---|---|---|
| Peter is entitled to paid holidays | | |
| Peter hires his own helpers | | |
| Peter takes substantial financial risks when undertaking work for XYZ plc | | |
| Peter does not have to rectify mistakes in his work at his own expense | | |

........................................................................

## Task 3.3

Emma is employed as a retail salesperson and provides you with the following information about what she has received from her employer:

(1)   Monthly salary of £2,000 paid on the first of each month until September 2020, with a 2% increase starting from 1 October 2020

(2)   Commission of £1,000 earned during a special sales event in March 2021, paid with the May 2021 salary

(3)   Employer's contribution of 5% of salary on 31 March 2021 to company's occupational pension scheme

(4)   Bonus of £1,200 received 30 April 2020, based on company's accounting profit for the year ended 31 March 2020

**For each item, show the amount that will be taxable in 2020/21:**

**Use whole numbers, and if the answer is zero, write 0.**

| Item | £ |
|---|---|
| Salary | |
| Commission | 0 |
| Employer's pension contribution | 0 |
| Bonus | 1200 |

## Task 3.4

**Show whether the following statement is true or false.**

Tips received by a tour guide from customers are not earnings.

| | ✓ |
|---|---|
| True | |
| False | ✓ |

## Task 3.5

A director of a company is entitled to a bonus for her employer's year ended 31 December 2020. The bonus is determined on 30 November 2020, credited to her director's account on 20 December 2020 and is actually paid to her on 6 January 2021.

**The date of receipt of the bonus for employment income purposes is: (insert date as xx/xx/xxxx)**

|  |
|  |

## Task 3.6

Mo was provided with a petrol engine car by her employer on 6 August 2020 which was first registered in August 2020. The car cost the employer £13,500 and the list price of the car was £15,000. The car's $CO_2$ emissions were 147 g/km.

**(a)    The cost of the car in the taxable benefit computation is:**

| £ |  |
|---|---|

**(b)    The percentage used in the taxable benefit computation is:**

|  | % |
|---|---|

**(c)    The taxable benefit on the provision of the car is:**

| £ |  |
|---|---|

## Task 3.7

Frank was provided with a new diesel engine car with a list price of £25,000 on 6 June 2020 (first registered in May 2020). The firm paid for all fuel (£2,300) without requiring any payment by Frank for fuel for private use. However, he was required to pay the firm £35 per month for the private use of the car itself. The car has $CO_2$ emissions of 143 g/km and did not meet the RDE2 emissions standards.

**(a)    The taxable benefit on the provision of the car is:**

| £ |  |
|---|---|

**(b)    The taxable benefit on the provision of fuel is:**

| £ |  |
|---|---|

## Task 3.8

Julian is provided with a company car for business and private use throughout 2020/21. The car had a list price of £11,500 when bought new in December 2019 although the company paid £10,000 for the car after a dealer discount. It has a diesel engine, with $CO_2$ emissions of 72 g/km and does not meet the RDE2 emissions standards. The company pays for all running costs, including all fuel. Julian does not make any contribution for his private use of the car.

(a) **The cost of the car in the taxable benefit computation is:**

£ [ ]

(b) **The percentage used in the taxable benefit computation is:**

[ ] %

(c) **The taxable benefit in respect of the provision of fuel for private use is:**

£ [ ]

........................................................................................

## Task 3.9

Sarah works for XXM plc and is provided with a company car for business and private use throughout 2020/21 which was first registered in 2019.

The car has a diesel engine with $CO_2$ emissions of 194 g/km. It has a list price of £57,000. Sarah agreed to make a capital contribution of £6,000 towards the cost of the car. The company pays for all running costs, including all fuel. Sarah pays £50 a month towards the cost of private fuel – the actual cost of private fuel is about £90 a month.

(a) **Tick to show which percentage is used in the taxable benefit computation.**

| | ✓ |
|----|----|
| 27 | |
| 37 | |
| 43 | |
| 47 | |

**(b)** **The taxable benefit in respect of the provision of the car is:**

£ [                    ]

**(c)** **The taxable benefit in respect of the provision of the fuel for private use is:**

£ [                    ]

## Task 3.10

Francine is employed by Bale plc as a delivery driver and is supplied with a van, which she parks overnight at home. She uses the van to drive to the company's depot to pick up packages but otherwise is not allowed to use the van for her own private purposes. The company provides fuel for the van. The cost of fuel for driving the van from her home to the depot is £500 for 2020/21.

**Tick to show the taxable benefit for Francine in respect of the van for 2020/21.**

|        | ✓ |
|--------|---|
| £3,490 |   |
| £4,156 |   |
| £666   |   |
| Nil    |   |

## Task 3.11

A camera costing £200 is bought by an employer for the private use of an employee on 6 April 2019. The camera is purchased by the employee for £50 on 6 April 2020, when its market value is £120.

**The taxable benefit for 2020/21 is:**

£ [                    ]

## Task 3.12

On 6 April 2020 an employer made a loan of £50,000 to an employee. The employee repaid £20,000 on 6 December 2020. The remaining £30,000 was outstanding at 5 April 2021. Interest paid during the year was £825. The official rate of interest was 2.25% throughout 2020/21.

**(a)** **Using the average method, the taxable benefit for 2020/21 is:**

£ 

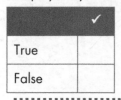

**(b)** **Using the alternative method, the taxable benefit for 2020/21 is:**

£ 

## Task 3.13

**Tick to show whether the following statement is true or false.**

If a loan of £7,000 to an employee is written-off and this is the only loan to the employee by the employer, there is no taxable benefit.

|  | ✓ |
|---|---|
| True |  |
| False |  |

## Task 3.14

**(a)** Vimal is given the use of a new television, costing £1,000, by his employer on 1 January 2019. Vimal subsequently buys the television from his employer for £100 on 1 January 2021 when it is worth £300.

**The taxable benefit for 2020/21 is:**

£ 

**(b)** The television is used to keep Vimal entertained when living at 3 Sims Court, London EC1, a flat provided by his employer. The flat cost £125,000 five years ago when Vimal moved in, but due to a slump in property prices is now only worth £90,000. It has an annual value of £3,000. The official rate of interest is 2.25%.

**The taxable benefit for 2020/21 is:**

£

## Task 3.15

Giles receives a salary of £25,000 and has received the following benefits from his employer throughout 2020/21:

(1)    Free medical insurance – the cost to the company is £385 per annum, although if Giles had taken this out privately, he would have to pay £525.

(2)    A watch worth £500 to celebrate Giles having worked for the company for 20 years.

(3)    A newspaper allowance of £20 per month.

Giles receives no income other than employment income.

**The total taxable benefits for 2020/21 are:**

£

## Task 3.16

Rita, a fashion designer for Daring Designs Ltd, was relocated from London to Manchester on 6 April 2020. Her annual salary is £48,000. She was reimbursed relevant relocation expenditure of £12,000. She was immediately provided with a house with an annual value of £4,000, for which her employer paid an annual rent of £3,500. Rita's employer provided ancillary services for the house in 2020/21 as follows:

|  | £ |
| --- | --- |
| Electricity | 700 |
| Gas | 1,200 |
| Water | 500 |
| Council tax | 1,300 |
| Property repairs | 3,500 |

The house had been furnished by Daring Designs Ltd immediately prior to Rita's occupation, at a cost of £30,000. On 6 October 2020 Rita bought all of the furniture from Daring Designs Ltd for £20,000 when its market value was £25,000.

Daring Designs Limited had made an interest-free loan to Rita in 2019 of £10,000. No part of the loan has been repaid. Assume the official rate of interest is 2.25%.

**(a)    The taxable benefit arising in respect of the accommodation provided for Rita in 2020/21 and purchase of the furniture is:**

£

**(b)** The taxable benefit arising in respect of the relocation expenses is:

£ [            ]

**(c)** The taxable benefit arising in respect of the interest free loan in 2020/21 is:

£ [            ]

## Task 3.17

Jon's employer provided him with a flat throughout 2020/21. The employer had bought the flat for £97,000 on 1 April 2018. The annual value of the flat is £800. Jon pays £100 a month to his employer for the use of the flat.

**Tick to show the total taxable accommodation benefit for 2020/21.**

|  | ✓ |
|---|---|
| £800 |  |
| £1,295 |  |
| £95 |  |
| £495 |  |

## Task 3.18

Petra uses her own car for business travel and her employer reimburses her 35p per mile. In 2020/21 Petra drove 13,000 business miles.

**Tick to show what is Petra's taxable benefit or allowable expense in respect of the business mileage.**

|  | ✓ |
|---|---|
| Taxable benefit of £700 |  |
| Allowable expense of £700 |  |
| Allowable expense of £1,300 |  |
| Taxable benefit of £4,550 |  |

## Task 3.19

**For an employee on an annual salary of £27,000, tick for each of the following benefits whether they would be taxable or exempt in 2020/21:**

| Item | Taxable | Exempt |
|---|---|---|
| Interest on loan of £2,000 (only loan provided) | | ✓ |
| Removal costs of £6,000 | | |
| Use of pool car | | |
| Reimbursement of business expenses | | |
| One staff party costing £100 per head | | |
| Accommodation provided to employee who is not required to live in it for the performance of employment | | |
| Provision of parking space at work | | |
| Additional costs of home-working of £6 per week | | |
| Non-cash long service award of £800 for 22 years of service | | |
| Accommodation provided to a caretaker for proper performance of his employment duties | | |
| Work related training | | |
| Provision of second mobile phone | | |

## Task 3.20

Selina is employed by JKL Ltd. She gives you the following information about money she has received from her employer, and expenditure that she has incurred in relation to her employment in 2020/21:

(1) Annual salary £30,000

(2) Reimbursed business expenses of £600

(3) Employee's contribution of 8% of salary to company's occupational pension scheme

(4) Membership of professional body of £150 paid by Selina

(5) Membership of fitness club of £300 paid by Selina – she often uses the club to meet new clients

(6)    £50 donation to charity each month under the payroll deduction scheme

(7)    £1,500 expenditure on smart clothes to wear to client meetings

(8)    A mobile telephone which Selina uses to speak to clients only.

**Using the proforma layout provided, compute Selina's employment income for 2020/21. If an expense is not allowable or a payment is non-taxable enter 0. Both brackets and minus signs can be used to indicate negative numbers (the expenses). Fill in all of the unshaded boxes.**

| | £ |
|---|---|
| Salary | |
| Less   allowable expenses: | |
|     reimbursed expenses | |
|     pension contribution | |
|     professional body membership | |
|     fitness club membership | |
|     charitable donation | |
|     clothing | |
|     Mobile telephone | |
| Employment income 2020/21 | |

## Task 3.21

Lewis is required by his employer to move from Truro to Manchester.

**The maximum amount of relocation expenses that his employer can pay without a taxable benefit arising is:**

£ [ ]

## Task 3.22

In 2020/21 Dave earns £20,000 a year in his employment with BCD plc, and also receives dividend income of £6,300 from the company.

**Tick to show the maximum pension contribution that Dave can make in 2020/21, on which he can obtain tax relief.**

|  | ✓ |
|---|---|
| £3,600 |  |
| £20,000 |  |
| £26,300 |  |
| £24,300 |  |

## Task 3.23

Zara works for KJ Ltd. She incurs the following travelling expenses in 2020/21:

|  | £ |
|---|---|
| Travel from her home in Preston to her workplace in Manchester | 1,500 |
| Travel to meet clients | 300 |
| Travel from her home in Preston to a temporary workplace in Birmingham (temporary period is 18 months) | 1,800 |

**Zara's qualifying travel expenses for 2020/21 are:**

£ [ ]

## Task 3.24

**Tick to show how the payroll deduction scheme for occupational pensions works.**

|  | ✓ |
|---|---|
| The employer deducts the contribution after calculating income tax under PAYE. | |
| The employer deducts basic rate tax from the contribution and the employee gets higher rate relief by extending the basic rate band in the tax computation. | |
| The employer deducts the contribution before calculating income tax under PAYE. | |
| The employer deducts basic rate tax from the contribution and there is no higher rate tax relief. | |

## Task 3.25

**Tick to show how tax relief is given on an employee's charitable donations made via Payroll Giving.**

|  | ✓ |
|---|---|
| The donation is paid net of basic rate tax, and higher rate tax relief is obtained by extending the basic rate band. | |
| The donation is deducted from employment income as an allowable expense before tax is calculated under PAYE. | |

## Task 3.26

**This style of task is human marked in the live assessment.**

You have received the following email from your client Martin Wilkes:

| | |
|---|---|
| **From:** | MartinWilkes@boxmail.net |
| **To:** | AATStudent@boxmail.net |
| **Sent:** | 12 March 2021 10:24 |
| **Subject:** | Car |

I have just received a promotion, and my employer is offering me a brand new company car for business and personal use from 6 April 2021. My employer is getting a good deal on the car because I looked up the list price, which is £18,000, but they are only paying £14,000 after a discount from the dealer. I also noted that the car has $CO_2$ emissions of 142 g/km.

My employer will pay all the running costs of the car and will also provide all the fuel. I will pay £20 a month towards private fuel, but I think that my actual private fuel used would cost about £50.

Can you please explain all of the taxation aspects of the provision of this car as a taxable benefit? Is there any other information that you need to know?

Thanks,

Martin Wilkes

**Reply to Martin's email, explaining to him the various taxation aspects that can apply to the provision of the car. Assume rates stay unchanged for future years.**

| | |
|---|---|
| **From:** | AATStudent@boxmail.net |
| **To:** | MartinWilkes@boxmail.net |
| **Sent:** | 14 March 2021 12:29 |
| **Subject:** | Car |

# Chapter 4 – Property income

## Task 4.1

Simran rents out a furnished house from 1 July 2020. The rent is £500 per month, payable on the first day of each month. She has chosen to use the accruals basis for her property profits. She incurs the following costs relating to the rental:

| | £ |
|---|---|
| Electricity for 1 July 2020 to 31 March 2021 | 1,200 |
| Water rates for 1 July 2020 to 31 March 2021 | 500 |
| Insurance for 1 July 2020 to 30 June 2021 | 360 |
| Replacement furniture purchased on 1 August 2020 | 400 |

**Tick to show what Simran's property income for 2020/21 is.**

| | ✓ |
|---|---|
| £2,630 | |
| £2,540 | |
| £2,040 | |
| £2,130 | |

## Task 4.2

Julie received the following property income during 2020/21:

(1) Annual rental of £6,300 (payable in advance) from a furnished flat first let on 6 August 2020. During the tax year the Julie spent £420 on replacement furniture and allowable expenses of £660.

(2) £3,500 from renting out her garage in London for parking.

**What amount of taxable property income does Julie have for 2020/21?**

| £ | |
|---|---|

## Task 4.3

Zelda lets out a house and uses the accruals basis to calculate her profits. Her accrued income and allowable expenses are as follows:

|  | Income £ | Expenses £ |
|---|---|---|
| 2018/19 | 6,000 | 10,000 |
| 2019/20 | 8,000 | 5,500 |
| 2020/21 | 10,000 | 4,000 |

Zelda's property income for 2020/21 is:

£

## Task 4.4

On 1 October 2020 Nitin buys a badly dilapidated house for £350,000. During October 2020, he spends £40,000 on making the house habitable. He lets it, fully furnished, for £3,600 a month from 1 November 2020, but the tenant leaves on 31 January 2021. A new tenant moves in on 1 March 2021, paying £4,000 a month rent.

Water rates are £195 for the period 1 October 2020 to 31 March 2021, payable by Nitin. He also pays buildings insurance of £480 for the period from 1 October 2020 to 30 September 2021. He spends £1,461 on replacement carpets in February 2021. Nitin uses the accruals basis to calculate his property profits.

**Nitin's property income for 2020/21 is:**

£

## Task 4.5

Sinead starts to let out property on 1 July 2020.

(1) On 1 July 2020, she lets a house which she has owned for several years. The tenant is required to pay annual rent of £8,000, quarterly in advance. The house is let unfurnished. She incurs total allowable expenses of £1,200 in relation to this letting.

(2) On 1 December 2020, she lets out a house which she has bought. The tenant pays rent of £450 per month, payable on the first of each month. The house is let unfurnished. She incurs total allowable expenses of £2,000 in relation to this letting.

**Sinead's property income for 2020/21 is:**

| £ | |
|---|---|

## Task 4.6

In 2020/21, Sally makes a property income loss of £(5,000) on letting out Red Roofs, and property income profit of £3,000 on letting out Green Acres. Sally also has employment income of £20,000 in 2020/21.

**Sally can obtain loss relief by: (tick ONE box)**

| | ✓ |
|---|---|
| Setting the loss of £(5,000) against her employment income in 2020/21 | |
| Carrying forward the loss of £(5,000) against property income in 2021/22 | |
| Setting the loss of £(5,000) first against the profit of £3,000 in 2020/21 and then carrying forward the balance of £(2,000) against property income in 2021/22 | |
| Setting the loss of £(5,000) first against the profit of £3,000 in 2020/21 and then setting the balance of £(2,000) against employment income in 2020/21 | |

## Task 4.7

Pierce Jones owns a flat that he rents out for £500 per calendar month, payable on the first day of each month. The property is let furnished. His other expenses for 2020/21 were:

| | £ |
|---|---|
| Electricity and gas | 1,200 |
| Water rates | 400 |
| Purchase of a television (not a replacement) | 1,300 |
| Repairs to roof following storm damage | 3,200 |
| Insurance | 250 |

**What is his assessable property income for 2020/21?**

| £ | |
|---|---|

## Task 4.8

**(a)  Property income is assessed as: (tick ONE box)**

| | ✓ |
|---|---|
| Non-savings income | |
| Savings income | |
| Dividend income | |
| Not taxable | |

**(b)  Property income is taxed at: (tick ONE box)**

| | ✓ |
|---|---|
| 20/40/45% | |
| 10/20/40/45% | |
| 0/7.5/32.5/38.1% | |
| 0/20/40/45% | |

# Chapter 5 – National insurance

## Task 5.1

In 2020/21 Steve received the following from his employer. For each item, indicate whether it would be subject to Class 1 Employee, Class 1 Employer, Class 1A National Insurance or none of these by ticking all the boxes that apply:

|  | Class 1 Employee | Class 1 Employer | Class 1A | None |
|---|---|---|---|---|
| Salary |  |  |  |  |
| Company car |  |  |  |  |
| Mileage expenses paid at 35p per mile |  |  |  |  |
| Bonus |  |  |  |  |
| Department store vouchers |  |  |  |  |
| Reimbursed travel expenses |  |  |  |  |
| Private gym membership |  |  |  |  |

## Task 5.2

In 2020/21 Iain received the following from his employer. Salary £27,000 (paid monthly), company car £3,000 taxable benefit, bonus in December 2020 of £2,000.

**Show the national insurance that would be payable on these amounts.**

(a)  **Class 1 Employee**

£ _____

(b)  **Class 1 Employer**

£ _____

(c)  **Class 1A**

£ _____

## Task 5.3

Ann was paid an annual salary of £45,000 in 2020/21 and her employer provided her with a laptop for personal use only. The taxable benefit for use of the laptop would be £300.

**Please complete the following sentence using the picklists below.**

**Ann and her employer would be liable to** [____▼] **on** [____▼] **and** [____▼] **on** [____▼]

**Picklist 1:**

Class 1 Employee

Class 1 Employer

Class 1 Employee and Employer

Class 1A

**Picklist 2:**

£45,300

£45,000

£300

£nil

........................................................

## Task 5.4

**Tick to show whether the following statement is true or false.**

50p per mile paid to an employee for mileage would be exempt from national insurance.

| | ✓ |
|---|---|
| True | |
| False | |

........................................................

## Task 5.5

**Tick to show whether the following statement is true or false.**

Class 1A NIC is payable on vouchers given to an employee as a reward for working overtime.

| | ✓ |
|---|---|
| True | |
| False | |

## Task 5.6

Wise Ltd has one employee, Freya, who is also a director of the company. In 2020/21 Wise Ltd pays Freya an annual salary of £37,000.

**What are the Class 1 employer contributions payable by Wise Ltd for 2020/21?**

**Please tick ONE box only.**

| | ✓ |
|---|---|
| £nil | |
| £5,106 | |
| £3,893 | |
| £3,795 | |

## Task 5.7

**What national insurance contributions are payable by employers and employees on a company car benefit? Please choose from the picklist below:**

| | |
|---|---|
| Employers | ▼ |
| Employees | ▼ |

**Picklist:**

Class 1A
Class 1 Employee
Class 1 Employer
None

# Chapter 6 – Chargeable gains

## Task 6.1

**Fill in the boxes.**

For the gain on the disposal of a capital asset to be a chargeable gain there must be a chargeable

```
[                    ]
```

of a chargeable

```
[                    ]
```

by a chargeable

```
[                    ]
```

## Task 6.2

**Tick to show whether the following assets are chargeable assets or exempt assets for capital gains tax.**

| Item | Chargeable asset | Exempt asset |
|------|------------------|--------------|
| Car | | |
| A plot of land | | |
| Jewellery | | |
| Premium bonds | | |
| Government stock ('gilts') | | |

BPP
LEARNING MEDIA

## Task 6.3

**Tick to show which ONE of the following is not a chargeable disposal for capital gains purposes.**

| | ✓ |
|---|---|
| The gift of an asset | |
| The sale of part of an asset | |
| The transfer of an asset on death | |
| The sale of the whole of an asset | |

## Task 6.4

Kate purchased a freehold property for £40,000. Kate then spent £5,000 on a new roof for the property as the old roof was storm damaged prior to acquisition. She sold the property for £90,100 on 15 March 2021. Kate had not made any other disposals during 2020/21.

**What is Kate's taxable gain for 2020/21?**

| | ✓ |
|---|---|
| £32,800 | |
| £37,800 | |
| £45,100 | |
| £50,100 | |

## Task 6.5

In November 2020, Lenny made chargeable gains of £20,400 and allowable losses of £3,560. He made no other disposals during 2020/21 and is a higher rate taxpayer.

**(a) Lenny's capital gains tax liability for 2020/21 is:**

£ [          ]

**(b) Lenny's capital gains tax liability is payable by: (insert date as xx/xx/xxxx)**

[          ]

## Task 6.6

In November 2020, Larry made chargeable gains of £25,400 and allowable losses of £5,200. He made no other disposals during 2020/21. He has £4,000 of his basic rate tax band remaining.

**Larry's capital gains tax liability for 2020/21 is:**

£ [                    ]

## Task 6.7

Laura made chargeable gains of £5,400 in July 2020 and £17,500 in November 2020. In May 2020 she made allowable losses of £2,000. Laura has taxable income of £32,435 for 2020/21.

**Laura's capital gains tax liability for 2020/21 is:**

£ [                    ]

## Task 6.8

Lisa made chargeable gains of £28,000 in December 2020. She made no other disposals in the year. Her taxable income for 2020/21 was £31,535.

**Lisa's capital gains tax liability for 2020/21 is:**

£ [                    ]

## Task 6.9

Darren bought a 3-acre plot of land for £150,000. He sold two acres of the land at auction for £240,000. His disposal costs were £3,000. The market value of the one remaining acre at the date of sale was £60,000.

**(a)    The cost of the land sold is:**

£ [                ]

**(b)    The chargeable gain on sale is:**

£ [                ]

## Task 6.10

**Tick to show how a taxpayer will pay the capital gains tax due for 2020/21.**

|  | ✓ |
|---|---|
| The full amount will be paid on 31 January 2022 |  |
| The full amount will be paid on 31 January 2021 |  |
| Payments on account will be made on 31 January and 31 July 2021, with the balance being paid on 31 January 2022 |  |
| Payments on account will be made on 31 January and 31 July 2020, with the balance being paid on 31 January 2021 |  |

## Task 6.11

Mattheus made gains of £20,100 and losses of £7,000 in 2020/21. He has losses brought forward of £5,000.

**The losses to carry forward to 2021/22 are (do not use brackets or a minus sign):**

£ 

## Task 6.12

Mike inherited a valuable painting from a distant uncle in November 2009. The painting had cost his uncle £5,000 in January 2001 and was valued at £9,000 at the date of his death. Luckily for Mike, when he sold it in December 2020, the proceeds were £16,000.

**Mike's chargeable gain on sale is:**

£

## Task 6.13

Luke sells one acre of land in August 2020 for £25,000. His disposal costs were £2,500. He had bought four acres of land for £15,000. The market value of the remaining land was £50,000 at the date of sale. The acquisition costs of the four acres of land were £1,500.

**Luke's chargeable gain on sale is:**

| £ | |
|---|---|

## Task 6.14

### Tick to show whether the following statement is True or False.

If an individual has allowable losses brought forward, these are set off after the annual exempt amount.

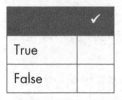

| | ✓ |
|---|---|
| True | |
| False | |

## Task 6.15

James has the following gains and losses arising from disposals of chargeable assets:

| Tax year | 2018/19 | 2019/20 | 2020/21 |
|---|---|---|---|
| Gains | £2,000 | £4,000 | £14,000 |
| Losses | £(14,000) | £(2,000) | £(2,000) |

**The maximum allowable loss carried forward to 2021/22 will be:**

| £ | |
|---|---|

## Task 6.16

Mary is married to Mike. They have a daughter, Beatrice. Mike has a sister, Susan who is married to Simon. Susan and Simon have a daughter called Sarah.

**Tick which ONE of the following is not a connected person in relation to Mary.**

|  | ✓ |
|---|---|
| Beatrice | |
| Susan | |
| Simon | |
| Sarah | |

## Task 6.17

Joanne gives an asset to her son in September 2020. There was an allowable loss on the disposal of £(3,000). Joanne also gave an asset to her daughter in October 2020. There was a chargeable gain of £5,000 on this disposal.

**Tick to show whether the following statement is True or False.**

The loss of £(3,000) can be set against the gain of £5,000.

|  | ✓ |
|---|---|
| True | |
| False | |

## Task 6.18

Xena bought a vase for £1,500 and sold it in October 2020 for £6,500, incurring expenses of sale of £130.

**Her chargeable gain on sale is:**

| £ | |
|---|---|

## Task 6.19

Jolyon purchased a gold ring for £7,000. He sold it in January 2021 for £3,000. The expenses of sale were £125.

**Jolyon's allowable loss is (do not use brackets or a minus sign):**

| £ | |
|---|---|

## Task 6.20

Rowenna bought a necklace for £4,000. She sold it in September 2020 for £5,500.

**Tick to show whether the following statement is True or False.**

Rowenna has a chargeable gain on sale of £1,500.

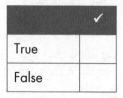

| | ✓ |
|---|---|
| True | |
| False | |

## Task 6.21

Gilda purchased a picture for £3,500 and sold it in September 2020 for £7,500, incurring £300 expenses of sale.

**Tick to show the chargeable gain on sale of the picture.**

| | ✓ |
|---|---|
| £1,200 | |
| £2,200 | |
| £2,500 | |
| £3,700 | |

## Task 6.22

Mark purchased an antique vase for £9,000. He sold the vase in August 2020 at auction for £4,500 net of auctioneer's fees of £500.

**Mark's allowable loss is (both minus signs and brackets can be used to indicate negative numbers):**

£ [          ]

..................................................................................................

# Chapter 7 – Share disposals

## Task 7.1

On 17 January 2021 Lionel sold 10,000 ordinary shares in Old plc. He had originally purchased 12,000 shares in Old plc on 10 May 2008 and purchased another 8,000 shares on 24 January 2021.

**Tick to show how Lionel's disposal of 10,000 shares in Old plc will be matched with his acquisitions.**

| | ✓ |
|---|---|
| Against 10,000 of the shares purchased on 10 May 2008 | |
| Against 5,000 of the shares purchased on 24 January 2021 and then against 5,000 of the shares purchased on 10 May 2008 | |
| Against 10,000 of the total shareholding of 20,000 shares | |
| Against the 8,000 shares purchased on 24 January 2021 and then against 2,000 of the shares purchased on 10 May 2008 | |

## Task 7.2

Mr Stevens sold 5,000 ordinary shares in JKL plc for £20,000 on 10 August 2020. He bought 6,000 shares in JKL plc for £9,000 on 15 July 2018 and another 1,000 shares for £4,200 on 16 August 2020.

**His net chargeable gain on sale is:**

£ [            ]

## Task 7.3

**This style of task is human marked in the live assessment.**

Eloise's dealings in Moo plc were as follows:

|  | No. of shares | Cost/proceeds £ |
|---|---|---|
| 10 February 2001 | 12,000 | 18,000 |
| 20 September 2008 | Bonus issue of 1 for 4 | Nil |
| 15 March 2021 | (2,000) | 8,000 |

**Using the proforma layout provided, calculate Eloise's gain on sale. Fill in all the unshaded boxes and if the answer is zero insert '0'. Both minus signs and brackets can be used to indicate negative numbers.**

**Share pool**

|  | No. of shares | Cost £ |
|---|---|---|
| 10 February 2001 |  |  |
| 20 September 2008 Bonus 1:4 |  |  |
|  |  |  |
| 15 March 2021 Disposal |  |  |
|  |  |  |

**Gain on sale**

|  | £ |
|---|---|
| Proceeds |  |
| Less cost |  |
| Gain |  |

## Task 7.4

**This style of task is human marked in the live assessment.**

Mark sold 10,000 of his shares in AC plc on 4 November 2020 for £60,000. The shares had been acquired as follows:

|  | No. of shares | Cost £ |
|---|---|---|
| 9 December 2001 | 12,000 | 4,400 |
| 12 October 2005 (Rights issue 1:3 at £5) | | |
| 10 November 2020 | 2,000 | 11,500 |

**Calculate Mark's total chargeable gain on sale. All workings must be shown. If the answer is zero insert '0'. Both minus signs and brackets can be used to indicate negative numbers.**

|  |  |  |
|---|---|---|
|  |  |  |
|  |  |  |
|  |  |  |
|  |  |  |
|  |  |  |
|  |  |  |
|  |  |  |
|  |  |  |
|  |  |  |
|  |  |  |
|  |  |  |
|  |  |  |
|  |  |  |
|  |  |  |
|  |  |  |

## Task 7.5

**This style of task is human marked in the live assessment.**

Darren sold 700,000 of his shares in R plc on 24 September 2020 for £3,675,000. The shares had been acquired as follows:

| | No. of shares | Cost £ |
|---|---|---|
| 2 June 2006 | 500,000 | 960,000 |
| 1 December 2011 (Bonus issue 3:2) | | |

**Calculate Darren's total chargeable gain on sale. All workings must be shown. If the answer is zero insert '0'. Both minus signs and brackets can be used to indicate negative numbers.**

| | | |
|---|---|---|
| | | |
| | | |
| | | |
| | | |
| | | |
| | | |
| | | |
| | | |
| | | |
| | | |
| | | |
| | | |
| | | |
| | | |
| | | |
| | | |
| | | |

# Chapter 8 – Private residence relief

## Task 8.1

Nicole is selling her main residence, which she has owned for 25 years. She lived in the house for the first eight years and nine months of ownership, let the property for the next five years whilst she was posted abroad by her employer, returned to live in the house for the next two years, and then moved out for the remainder of her period of ownership.

**Tick to show what fraction of her gain will be exempt under the private residence exemption.**

|            | ✓ |
|------------|---|
| 16.5/25    |   |
| 10.75/25   |   |
| 15.75/25   |   |
| 8.5/25     |   |

## Task 8.2

Mr Kitch bought a house in 2006 and lived in it until June 2020 when he moved out to live with his girlfriend. He sold the house in December 2020 and made a gain of £30,000.

**The whole gain will be covered by private residence relief.**

|       | ✓ |
|-------|---|
| True  |   |
| False |   |

## Task 8.3

Mr Fox bought a house on 1 August 2001 for £50,000. He lived in the house until 31 July 2004. He then went abroad to work as a self-employed engineer until 31 July 2009. He lived in the house again until 31 January 2010, when he moved out.

Mr Fox sold the house on 31 July 2020 for £180,000.

**Using the proforma layout provided, calculate the chargeable gain on sale.**

|  | £ |
|---|---|
| Proceeds |  |
| Less cost |  |
| Gain before PRR |  |
| Less PRR exemption |  |
| Chargeable gain |  |

## Task 8.4

Jose purchased a house and lived in it for three years. The house was then unoccupied for five years when he was required to work abroad in Spain. He moved back to the UK and lived in the house for two years before moving out to live with his girlfriend. The house was unoccupied for four years before he moved back to the house for the final six months of ownership.

**Tick to show what fraction of his gain will be exempt under the private residence exemption.**

|  | ✓ |
|---|---|
| 13.75/14.5 |  |
| 13.5/14.5 |  |
| 10.5/14.5 |  |
| 10.75/14.5 |  |

## Task 8.5

David purchased a house in 2006. He lived in the property for a year before going travelling for four years. He moved back to the property for five years before going to work abroad for his current employer. He sold the house in 2020 without returning to the property.

**All periods of absence will be covered by private residence relief.**

| | ✓ |
|---|---|
| True | |
| False | |

## Chapter 9 – Inheritance tax

### Task 9.1

Identify whether the following transfers will be treated as a **PET**, a **CLT** or exempt for Inheritance Tax purposes in 2020/21. Tick **ONE** box per transfer.

| | PET | CLT | Exempt |
|---|---|---|---|
| Gift of £100 cash to niece | | | |
| Gift of shares to a trust | | | |
| Payment of grandson's school fees out of income surplus to living requirements | | | |
| Gift of £5,000 to son on the occasion of his marriage | | | |
| Gift of £25,000 to friend | | | |
| Gift of classic car to spouse | | | |
| Gift of £10,000 to a trust | | | |

### Task 9.2

Norman died in May 2020. His estate was valued at £500,000. £100,000 was left to his cousin and the balance to his wife Maureen. Neither Norman nor Maureen own any property.

**How much nil band would be available to Maureen on her death?**

£ [          ]

## Task 9.3

Identify which of the following debts would be deductible and which would not be deductible in a death estate?

| | Deductible | Not deductible |
|---|---|---|
| Grocery bill | | |
| HM Revenue & Customs – income tax to death | | |
| Mortgage on home | | |
| Illegal gambling debt | | |

## Task 9.4

Tick to show whether the following statement is true or false.

PETs are subject to inheritance tax in both life and death.

| | ✔ |
|---|---|
| True | |
| False | |

## Task 9.5

Tick to show whether the following statement is true or false.

A £5,000 exemption is available on any gifts given on a marriage.

| | ✔ |
|---|---|
| True | |
| False | |

## Task 9.6

On 15 July 2020 Yvonne gave £500,000 to a trust for the benefit of her grandchildren. Yvette died on 27 December 2020.

**What are the due dates for inheritance tax to be paid on this transfer of value? (please tick ONE box only)**

| Lifetime tax | Death tax | ✓ |
|---|---|---|
| 31 January 2021 | 30 June 2021 | |
| 30 April 2021 | 30 June 2021 | |
| 31 January 2021 | 30 April 2021 | |
| 30 April 2021 | 30 April 2021 | |

........................................................................................

## Task 9.7

Bernard made a chargeable lifetime transfer of £260,000 (after exemptions) in August 2016. In November 2020, he gave £420,000 to a trust for the benefit of his son and daughter. Bernard agreed to pay any lifetime IHT due.

**How much inheritance tax will be payable by Bernard on transfer of value in November 2020? Please tick ONE box only.**

| | ✓ |
|---|---|
| £87,250 | |
| £69,800 | |
| £88,750 | |
| £22,250 | |

........................................................................................

## Task 9.8

Fred gives away shares in Fred Plc. On the date of transfer the shares were valued at 250–280p with marked bargains of 252, 276, 264 and 279.

**What is the value per share used in the IHT calculation? (show your answer in pence)**

|  | P |
|---|---|

........................................................................................

## Task 9.9

June gives 200 shares to her daughter – these shares are worth £3 each. June owned 500 shares prior to this transfer and the shares were worth £10 each. After the transfer June's remaining shares will be valued at £7.50 each.

**What is the diminution in value of June's estate?**

| £ | |
|---|---|

## Task 9.10

Amanda died on 30 September 2020. She left an estate valued at £1,225,000, including her house which was valued at £400,000. She left the house to her children, £200,000 to her husband Nick, and the residue of her estate to her sister Becky.

Amanda had made no gifts during her lifetime.

**What is the inheritance tax payable on Amanda's estate?**

**Please tick ONE box only.**

| | ✓ |
|---|---|
| £340,000 | |
| £210,000 | |
| £280,000 | |
| £290,000 | |

# Chapter 10 – The tax and ethical framework

## Task 10.1

**The tax year 2020/21 runs from: (insert dates as xx/xx/xxxx)**

|  |
| --- |
|  |

**until:**

|  |
| --- |
|  |

## Task 10.2

**Tick to show whether the following statement is true or false.**

Detailed regulations relating to tax law are contained in Statutory Instruments.

|  | ✓ |
| --- | --- |
| True |  |
| False |  |

## Task 10.3

**Tick to show who the UK tax system is administered by.**

|  | ✓ |
| --- | --- |
| Parliament |  |
| Her Majesty's Revenue & Customs (HMRC) |  |
| National Crime Agency (NCA) |  |
| HM Customs & Excise |  |

## Task 10.4

**If you are employed by a firm of accountants, and suspect that one of your clients may be engaged in money laundering, whom should you inform about your suspicions?**

|  | ✓ |
| --- | --- |
| HMRC | |
| Your firm's Money Laundering Reporting Officer | |
| National Crime Agency | |
| Tax Tribunal | |

## Task 10.5

**This style of task is human marked in the live assessment.**

One of your clients has expressed concern that his personal tax information may be disclosed to members of his family, who are also clients of your firm. He feels that this would compromise his right to privacy in his personal affairs.

**Write a note responding to this concern.**

## Task 10.6

**Tick to show in which TWO of the following situations an accountant is able to disclose information about a client without their permission.**

|  | ✓ |
|---|---|
| If the client is unwell and unable to respond to HMRC |  |
| If money laundering is suspected |  |
| Where it would be illegal not to disclose the information |  |
| If the information is requested from a 'connected person' |  |

## Task 10.7

**The five fundamental principles of professional ethics for AAT members are:**

Use the letters in the left column as a guide.

| I |  |
|---|---|
| O |  |
| Pc and dc |  |
| C |  |
| Pb |  |

## Task 10.8

**Tick to show who you should inform about your suspicions if you are a sole practitioner and suspect that one of your clients may be engaged in money laundering.**

|  | ✓ |
|---|---|
| HMRC |  |
| Another firm's Money Laundering Reporting Officer |  |
| National Crime Agency |  |
| Tax Tribunal |  |

## Task 10.9

**Tick to show whether the following statement is true or false.**

A non-UK resident individual is liable to pay income tax on their UK and overseas income

|  | ✓ |
|---|---|
| True | |
| False | |

........................................................................................

## Task 10.10

**This style of task is human marked in the live assessment.**

A client has received a tax refund of £12,000 from HMRC. They were not due this refund but have already spent the money and asked you not to inform HMRC of their mistake.

**What action should you take?**

........................................................................................

## Task 10.11

**Tick to show whether the following statement is true or false.**

Tax avoidance is illegal.

| | ✓ |
|---|---|
| True | |
| False | |

# Answer Bank

# Chapter 1

## Task 1.1

| | Non-savings income | Savings income | Dividend income |
|---|---|---|---|
| Trading income | ✓ | | |
| Dividend received from a company | | | ✓ |
| Property income | ✓ | | |
| Building society interest | | ✓ | |
| Bank interest | | ✓ | |
| Pension income | ✓ | | |
| Employment income | ✓ | | |
| Interest from government stock ('gilts') | | ✓ | |

## Task 1.2

**(a)** **Bank account interest £160**

| £ | 160 |
|---|---|

**(b)** **Premium bond prize £100**

| £ | 0 |
|---|---|

Premium bond prizes are exempt income.

**(c)** **Dividends £540**

| £ | 540 |
|---|---|

## Task 1.3

| | Gross | Net | Exempt |
|---|:---:|:---:|:---:|
| Bank interest | ✓ | | |
| Interest on an individual savings account (ISA) | | | ✓ |
| Employment income | | ✓ | |
| Interest from government stock ('gilts') | ✓ | | |

## Task 1.4

### Jonty's taxable income for 2020/21 is:

| £ | 26,373 |
|---|---|

| | Non-savings income £ | Savings income £ | Dividend income £ | Total £ |
|---|---|---|---|---|
| Earnings | 38,730 | | | |
| Building society interest | | 80 | | |
| Dividends | | | 63 | |
| Net income | 38,730 | 80 | 63 | 38,873 |
| Less personal allowance | (12,500) | | | (12,500) |
| Taxable income | 26,230 | 80 | 63 | 26,373 |

## Task 1.5

| | Non-savings income £ | Savings income £ | Total £ |
|---|---|---|---|
| Earnings | 15,665 | 0 | |
| Bank deposit interest | 0 | 457 | |
| Building society interest | 0 | 400 | |
| ISA interest | 0 | 0 | |
| Net income | 15,665 | 857 | 16,522 |
| Less personal allowance | (12,500) | 0 | (12,500) |
| Taxable income | 3,165 | 857 | 4,022 |

## Task 1.6

**(a)** **Hayley's net income for 2020/21 is:**

£ | 101,100

| | Non-savings income £ | Savings income £ | Dividend income £ | Total £ |
|---|---|---|---|---|
| Employment income | 95,000 | | | |
| Bank interest | | 1,600 | | |
| Dividends | | | 4,500 | |
| | | | | |
| Net income | 95,000 | 1,600 | 4,500 | 101,100 |

**Note.** ISA interest is exempt from income tax.

**(b)** **The personal allowance that Hayley is entitled to for 2020/21 is:**

£ | 11,950

|  | £ |
|---|---|
| Net income | 101,100 |
| Less income limit | (100,000) |
| Excess | 1,100 |
|  |  |
| Personal allowance | 12,500 |
| Less half excess | (550) |
|  | 11,950 |

## Task 1.7

**Max's personal allowance for 2020/21 is:**

£ | 6,500

|  | £ |
|---|---|
| Net income | 116,000 |
| Less Gift Aid donations (gross) | (4,000) |
| Adjusted net income | 112,000 |
| Less income limit | (100,000) |
| Excess | 12,000 |
|  |  |
| Personal allowance | 12,500 |
| Less half excess | (6,000) |
|  | 6,500 |

## Task 1.8

**(a)** **Gavin's net income for 2020/21 is:**

| £ | 26,700 |
|---|--------|

| | Non-savings income £ | Savings income £ | Dividend income £ | Total £ |
|---|---|---|---|---|
| Pension income | 19,300 | | | |
| Bank interest | | 2,000 | | |
| Dividends | | | 5,400 | |
| | | | | |
| Net income | 19,300 | 2,000 | 5,400 | 26,700 |

**Note.** Lottery winnings are exempt from income tax.

**(b)** **The personal allowance that Gavin is entitled to for 2020/21 is:**

| £ | 12,500 |
|---|--------|

## Task 1.9

**From 6 April 2020 the maximum an individual can invest for the tax year in an ISA is:**

| £ | 20,000 |
|---|--------|

## Task 1.10

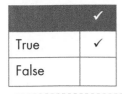

| | ✓ |
|---|---|
| True | ✓ |
| False | |

67

## Task 1.11

The statement is false. Damages received for both injury and death are always exempt from income tax.

|  | ✓ |
| --- | --- |
| True | |
| False | ✓ |

# Chapter 2

## Task 2.1

**(a)** **Guy's income tax liability is:**

| £ | 1,370 |
|---|-------|

|  | Non-savings income £ | Savings income £ | Total £ |
|---|---|---|---|
| Non-savings income | 12,850 |  |  |
| Bank interest |  | 7,500 |  |
| Net Income | 12,850 | 7,500 | 20,350 |
| PA | (12,500) |  | (12,500) |
| Taxable income | 350 | 7,500 | 7,850 |
| Tax: |  |  |  |
| NSI £350 × 20% |  | 70 |  |
| SI £1,000 × 0% (PSA) |  | 0 |  |
| SI £7,500 −1,000 = £6,500 × 20% |  | 1,300 |  |
| Income tax liability |  | 1,370 |  |

**(b) Guy's income tax liability is:**

£ | 11,040

| | Non-savings income £ | Savings income £ | Total £ |
|---|---|---|---|
| Non-savings income | 51,850 | | |
| Interest | | 7,500 | |
| Net income | 51,850 | 7,500 | 59,350 |
| PA | (12,500) | | (12,500) |
| Taxable income | 39,350 | 7,500 | 46,850 |
| Tax: | | | |
| NSI £37,500 × 20% | | 7,500 | |
| NSI £39,350 – 37,500 = £1,850 × 40% | | 740 | |
| SI £500 × 0% (PSA) | | 0 | |
| SI £7,500 – 500 = £7,000 × 40% | | 2,800 | |
| Income tax liability | | 11,040 | |

## Task 2.2

**(a)** **Non-savings income:**

| £ | 2,940 |
|---|-------|

**(b)** **Savings income:**

| £ | 235 |
|---|-----|

**(c)** **Dividend income:**

| £ | 0 |
|---|---|

**Note.** that 'taxable income' is the figure after the personal allowance.

| | Non-savings income £ | Savings income £ | Dividend income £ | Total £ |
|---|---|---|---|---|
| Taxable income | 14,700 | 2,176 | 1,766 | 18,642 |
| | | | | |
| Tax on non-savings income: | £14,700 × 20% | | 2,940 | |
| Tax on savings income: | | | | |
| £1,000 Basic Rate PSA | £1,000 × 0% | | 0 | |
| Balance of Savings Income | £1,176 × 20% | | 235 | |
| Tax on dividend income: | | | | |
| Covered by £2,000 DA | £1,766 × 0% | | 0 | |
| Income tax liability | | | 3,175 | |

## Task 2.3

| | ✓ |
|---|---|
| £150,000 | |
| £162,000 | |
| £165,000 | ✓ |
| £153,000 | |

Additional rate threshold £150,000 plus gross personal pension contribution of £15,000 (£12,000 × 100/80)

The answer of £150,000 is the additional rate threshold without adjustment. The answer £162,000 does not gross up the pension contribution. The answer £153,000 only adjusts the limit for the different between the gross and net pension contribution.

## Task 2.4

| | ✓ |
|---|---|
| £43,500 | |
| £37,500 | |
| £45,000 | ✓ |
| £30,000 | |

Basic rate band extended by the gross Gift Aid donation, ie £(6,000 × 100/80) = £7,500

£37,500 + £7,500 = £45,000

The answer £43,500 does not gross up the Gift Aid donation. The answer £37,500 is the basic rate threshold without adjustment. The answer £30,000 deducts the Gift Aid donation.

## Task 2.5

**(a)** **Katy's basic rate band for 2020/21 is:**

| £ | 42,500 |
|---|--------|

Basic rate band extended by the gross Gift Aid donation, ie £(4,000 × 100/80) = £5,000

£37,500 + £5,000

**(b)** **Katy's additional rate threshold for 2020/21 is:**

| £ | 155,000 |
|---|---------|

Additional rate threshold = £42,500 + £112,500 (or £150,000 + £5,000)

**(c)** **Katy's higher rate band for 2020/21 is:**

| £ | 112,500 |
|---|---------|

(£155,000 – £42,500)

....................................................................................

## Task 2.6

**(a)** **Ruth's personal savings allowance for 2020/21 is:**

| £ | 1,000 |
|---|-------|

Ruth is a basic rate taxpayer with ANI of <£50,000

**(b)** **Ruth's dividend allowance for 2020/21 is:**

| £ | 2,000 |
|---|-------|

The £2,000 dividend allowance is applicable to all taxpayers regardless of their marginal rate of tax.

....................................................................................

## Task 2.7

**Rachel's income tax liability for 2020/21 is:**

| £ | 2,170 |
|---|-------|

|  | £ |
|---|---|
| Net income | 24,350 |
| Less personal allowance | (12,500) |
| Taxable income | 11,850 |
|  |  |
| £1,000 × 0% (PSA) | 0 |
| £11,850 – 1,000 = £10,850 × 20% | 2,170 |
| Income tax liability | 2,170 |

## Task 2.8

**Richard's income tax payable for 2020/21 is:**

| £ | 3,510 |
|---|-------|

'Taxable income' is the figure after personal allowances have been deducted

|  | £ |
|---|---|
| Taxable income | 58,525 |

|  |  | £ |
|---|---|---|
| Tax | £37,500 × 20% | 7,500 |
|  | £13,500 (extended by £10,800 × 100/80) × 20% | 2,700 |
|  | £51,000 |  |
|  | £7,525 × 40% | 3,010 |
|  | £58,525 |  |

| | £ |
|---|---|
| Income tax liability | 13,210 |
| Less tax suffered at source (PAYE) | (9,700) |
| Income tax payable | 3,510 |

## Task 2.9

**(a)**

| | Non-savings income £ | Savings income £ | Dividend income £ | Total £ |
|---|---|---|---|---|
| Salary | 50,850 | 0 | 0 | |
| Dividend | 0 | 0 | 1,000 | |
| Bank deposit interest | 0 | 800 | 0 | |
| Net income | 50,850 | 800 | 1,000 | 52,650 |
| Less personal allowance | (12,500) | 0 | 0 | (12,500) |
| Taxable income | 38,350 | 800 | 1,000 | 40,150 |

The gross Gift Aid payment is £2,400 × 100/80 = £3,000.

The adjusted net income (52,650 – 3,000 Gift Aid) is less than £50,000 and so the £1,000 PSA applies.

**(b)** **John's income tax liability for 2020/21 is:**

| £ | 8,100 |
|---|---|

**(c)** **John's income tax payable for 2020/21 is:**

| £ | 100 |
|---|---|

75

|  | £ |
|---|---|
| Tax on non-savings income | |
| £37,500 × 20% | 7,500 |
| £850 × 20% | 170 |
| Gift aid extended the basic rate band to £37,500 + £3,000 (£2,400 × 100/80) = £40,500 | |
| Tax on savings income | |
| £800 × 0% (PSA) | 0 |
| Tax on dividend income | |
| £1,000 × 0% (covered by DA) | 0 |
| Income tax liability | 7,670 |
| Less PAYE (given) | (7,570) |
| Income tax payable | 100 |

## Task 2.10

**(a)**

|  | Non-savings income £ | Savings income £ | Dividend income £ | Total £ |
|---|---|---|---|---|
| Salary | 155,000 | 0 | 0 | |
| Dividend | 0 | 0 | 10,000 | |
| Bank deposit interest | 0 | 3,000 | 0 | |
| Net income | 155,000 | 3,000 | 10,000 | 168,000 |
| Less personal allowance | 0 | 0 | 0 | 0 |
| Taxable income | 155,000 | 3,000 | 10,000 | 168,000 |

The adjusted net income is in excess of £125,000 so the personal allowance is reduced to nil.

Additional rate tax payer and so the PSA does not apply.

**(b)** **Jean's income tax liability for 2020/21 is:**

| £ | 56,748 |
|---|--------|

**(c)** **Jean's income tax payable for 2020/21 is:**

| £ | 8,248 |
|---|-------|

|  | £ |
|---|---|
| Tax on non-savings income | |
| £37,500 × 20% | 7,500 |
| £10,000 (extended band: pension) £8,000 × 100/80 × 20% | 2,000 |
| £107,500 × 40% | 43,000 |
| Tax on savings income | |
| £3,000 × 40% | 1,200 |
| Tax on dividend income | |
| £2,000 × 0% (DA) | 0 |
| £160,000 (extended higher rate band £150,000 + £10,000) | |
| £8,000 × 38.1% | 3,048 |
| Income tax liability | 56,748 |
|  | |
| Less tax deducted at source | |
| PAYE (given) | (48,500) |
| Income tax payable | 8,248 |

**Note.** Additional rate threshold is increased by £10,000 to £160,000. Jean is not entitled to a personal savings allowance as she is an additional rate taxpayer.

••••••••••••••••••••••••••••••••••••••••••••••••••••••••••••••••••••••••••••••

## Task 2.11

| | Non-savings income £ | Savings income £ | Dividend income £ | Total £ |
|---|---|---|---|---|
| Pension income | 10,050 | | | |
| Bank interest | | 11,075 | | |
| Dividends | | | 10,000 | |
| Net income | 10,050 | 11,075 | 10,000 | 31,125 |
| Personal allowance | (10,050) | (2,450) | | (12,500) |
| Taxable income | Nil | 8,625 | 10,000 | 18,625 |
| Tax on savings income: | | | | |
| £1,000 × 0% (PSA) | | 0 | | |
| £7,625 (£8,625 – £1,000) × 20% | | 1,525 | | |
| Tax on dividend income: | | | | |
| £2,000 × 0% (DA) | | 0 | | |
| £8,000 × 7.5% | | 600 | | |
| Income tax liability | | 2,125 | | |

Adjusted net income ≤ £50,000 hence £1,000 PSA available.

Basic rate taxpayer therefore correct relief given at source so Gift Aid payment ignored.

## Task 2.12

| | Non-savings income £ | Savings income £ | Dividend income £ | Total £ |
|---|---|---|---|---|
| Trading income | 90,000 | | | |
| Bank interest | | 1,500 | | |
| Dividends | | | 15,000 | |
| Net income | 90,000 | 1,500 | 15,000 | 106,500 |
| Personal allowance (W) | (9,250) | | | (9,250) |
| Taxable income | 80,750 | 1,500 | 15,000 | 97,250 |
| Tax on non-savings income: | | | | |
| £37,500 × 20% | | 7,500 | | |
| £43,250 × 40% | | 17,300 | | |
| Tax on savings income: | | | | |
| £500 × 0% (PSA) | | 0 | | |
| £1,000 × 40% | | 400 | | |
| Tax on dividend income: | | | | |
| £2,000 × 0% (DA) | | 0 | | |
| £13,000 × 32.5% | | 4,225 | | |
| Income tax liability | | 29,425 | | |

(W) Jack has adjusted net income of £106,500 and therefore his personal allowance is restricted to: 12,500 – ((106,500 – 100,000) / 2) = £9,250.

**Note.** Jack is a higher rate tax payer and therefore only receives £500 PSA.

# Chapter 3

## Task 3.1

| | ✓ |
|---|---|
| True | |
| False | ✓ |

An employee has a contract of service.

## Task 3.2

| Factor | Contract of service | Contract for services |
|---|---|---|
| Peter is entitled to paid holidays | ✓ | |
| Peter hires his own helpers | | ✓ |
| Peter takes substantial financial risks when undertaking work for XYZ plc | | ✓ |
| Peter does not have to rectify mistakes in his work at his own expense | ✓ | |

## Task 3.3

| Item | £ |
|---|---|
| Salary | 24,280 |
| Commission | 0 |
| Employer's pension contribution | 0 |
| Bonus | 1,200 |

Salary paid on the first of each month, therefore received in 2020/21 as follows:

1 May 2020 to 1 September 2020 = 5 × £2,000 = £10,000

1 October 2020 to 1 April 2021 = 7 × £2,000 × 102% = £14,280

Salary = £10,000 + £14,280 = £24,280

## Task 3.4

|  | ✓ |
|---|---|
| True |  |
| False | ✓ |

Tips received by a tour guide from customers are earnings. Note that earnings can include money received other than from the employer.

····························································································

## Task 3.5

The date of receipt of the bonus for employment income purposes is:

| 20/12/2020 |
|---|

····························································································

## Task 3.6

(a) **The cost of the car in the taxable benefit computation is:**

| £ | 15,000 |
|---|---|

(b) **The percentage used in the taxable benefit computation is:**

| | 32 | % |
|---|---|---|

The $CO_2$ emissions of the car are 145g/km (rounded down to the nearest five).

Amount over baseline figure: 145 – 55 = 90 g/km

Divide 90 by 5 = 18

The taxable percentage is 14% + 18% = 32%

(c) **The taxable benefit on the provision of the car is:**

| £ | 3,200 |
|---|---|

32% × £15,000 × 8/12 (6 August 2020 to 5 April 2021)

····························································································

## Task 3.7

**(a)** **The taxable benefit on the provision of the car is:**

| £ | 6,942 |
|---|-------|

Round down $CO_2$ emissions to 140g/km

Amount above baseline: $140 - 55 = 85$g/km

Divide 85 by 5 = 17

Taxable % = 14% + 17% + 4% (diesel) = 35%

|  | £ |
|---|---|
| £25,000 × 35% × 10/12 | 7,292 |
| Less employee contribution (10 × £35) | (350) |
| Taxable benefit of car | 6,942 |

**(b)** **The taxable benefit on the provision of fuel is:**

| £ | 7,145 |
|---|-------|

£24,500 × 35% × 10/12 = £7,145

....................................................................

## Task 3.8

**(a)** **The cost of the car in the taxable benefit computation is:**

| £ | 11,500 |
|---|--------|

**(b)** **The percentage used in the taxable benefit computation is:**

| 23 | % |
|----|---|

Round down $CO_2$ emissions to 70g/km

Amount above baseline: $70 - 55 = 15$g/km

Divide 15 by 5 = 3

Taxable % = 14% + 3% + 4% (diesel) + 2% (pre-April 2020) = 23%

**(c)** **The taxable benefit in respect of the provision of fuel for private use is:**

| £ | 5,635 |
|---|-------|

£24,500 × 23%

....................................................................

## Task 3.9

**(a)** **The percentage used in the taxable benefit computation is:**

|  | ✓ |
|----|----|
| 27 |  |
| 37 | ✓ |
| 43 |  |
| 47 |  |

Round down $CO_2$ emissions to 190 g/km

Amount above baseline: 190 – 55 = 135 g/km

Divide 135 by 5 = 27

Taxable % = 14% + 27% + 4% (diesel) + 2% (pre-April 2020) = 47%, max 37%

The answer 27% is the amount to add to the basic taxable percentage. The answer 43% ignores the diesel supplement and the maximum rate. The answer 47% ignores the maximum rate.

**(b)** **The taxable benefit in respect of the provision of the car is:**

£ | 19,240

|  | £ |
|----|----|
| List price | 57,000 |
| Less capital contribution paid by employee (max) | (5,000) |
| Cost of car | 52,000 |
| Car benefit £52,000 × 37% | 19,240 |

**(c)** **The taxable benefit in respect of the provision of fuel for private use is:**

£ | 9,065

£24,500 × 37% = £9,065. There is no reduction for part reimbursement of private fuel.

## Task 3.10

| | ✓ |
|---|---|
| £3,490 | |
| £4,156 | |
| £666 | |
| Nil | ✓ |

There is no taxable benefit because there is no private use of the van – travel from home to work is not private use for vans.

The answer £3,490 is the private use benefit. The answer £4,156 is the private use benefit plus the private use fuel benefit. The answer £666 is the private use fuel benefit.

......................................................................................................

## Task 3.11

The taxable benefit for 2020/21 is:

| £ | 110 |
|---|---|

The benefit taxable in 2019/20 was 20% × £200 = £40

The benefit taxable in 2020/21 will be the greater of:

| | | £ | £ |
|---|---|---|---|
| (1) | Market value at acquisition by employee | 120 | |
| (2) | Original market value | 200 | |
| | Less benefit for use in 2019/20 | (40) | |
| | | 160 | |
| | Greater | | 160 |
| | Less price paid by employee | | (50) |
| | Taxable benefit 2020/21 | | 110 |

......................................................................................................

## Task 3.12

(a) **Using the average method, the taxable benefit for 2020/21 is:**

£ | 75

| | £ |
|---|---|
| 2.25% × (50,000 + 30,000)/2 | 900 |
| Less interest paid | (825) |
| Taxable benefit | 75 |

(b) **Using the alternative method, the taxable benefit for 2020/21 is:**

£ | 150

| | £ |
|---|---|
| £50,000 × 8/12 ×2.25% | 750 |
| (6 April 2020 to 5 December 2020) | |
| £30,000 × 4/12 × 2.25% | 225 |
| (6 December 2020 to 5 April 2021) | |
| | 975 |
| Less interest paid | (825) |
| Taxable benefit | 150 |

## Task 3.13

| | ✓ |
|---|---|
| True | |
| False | ✓ |

There is a taxable benefit of the amount of the loan written-off, however small the loan. The £10,000 limit only applies to the interest benefit.

## Task 3.14

### (a) The taxable benefit for 2020/21 is:

| £ | 650 |
|---|-----|

During 2020/21 Vimal will have a taxable benefit arising from the use of the asset:

£1,000 × 20% × 9/12 = £150

He will also have a benefit when the asset is sold to him at an undervalue.

This will be the higher of the MV at the date of the 'gift', and the original market value minus benefits assessed so far, less his £100 contribution.

|  | £ | £ |
|---|---|---|
| Market value at date of gift |  | 300 |
| Original market value |  | 1,000 |
| Assessed re use: |  |  |
| 2018/19: £1,000 × 20% × 3/12 | 50 |  |
| 2019/20: £1,000 × 20% | 200 |  |
| 2020/21: £1,000 × 20% × 9/12 | 150 |  |
|  |  | (400) |
|  |  | 600 |
| ie Higher value used |  | 600 |
| Less Vimal's contribution |  | (100) |
|  |  | 500 |
| His total benefit (for both use and 'gift') in 2020/21 will therefore be |  | 650 |

**(b)** **The taxable benefit for 2020/21 is:**

£ | 4,125

The taxable benefit for use of the flat is calculated as follows:

| | £ |
|---|---|
| Annual value | 3,000 |
| £(125,000 – 75,000) × 2.25% (expensive accommodation) | 1,125 |
| Taxable benefit | 4,125 |

The original cost is used, not the value now.

## Task 3.15

The total taxable benefits for 2020/21 are:

£ | 625

| | £ |
|---|---|
| Medical insurance (cost to employer) | 385 |
| Non-cash long service award (up to £50 × 20 years = £1,000) | 0 |
| Newspaper allowance (12 × £20) | 240 |
| Taxable benefits | 625 |

## Task 3.16

(a) **The taxable benefit arising in respect of the accommodation provided for Rita in 2020/21 and purchase of the furniture is:**

| £ | 21,200 |
|---|--------|

| | £ |
|---|---|
| Annual value (higher than rent paid) | 4,000 |
| Electricity | 700 |
| Gas | 1,200 |
| Water | 500 |
| Council tax | 1,300 |
| Repairs | 3,500 |
| Furniture (20% × £30,000 × 6/12) | 3,000 |
| Purchase of furniture (W) | 7,000 |
| | 21,200 |

**Working** Purchase of furniture

Benefit is the **higher** of:

| | | £ |
|---|---|---|
| (1) | Cost | 30,000 |
| | Less taxed for use of furniture (20% × £30,000 × 6/12) | (3,000) |
| | | 27,000 |
| | Less amount paid by Rita | (20,000) |
| | | 7,000 |
| (2) | Market value | 25,000 |
| | Less amount paid | (20,000) |
| | | 5,000 |

**(b)** **The taxable benefit arising in respect of the relocation expenses is:**

| £ | 4,000 |
|---|-------|

£12,000 – £8,000

**(c)** **The taxable benefit arising in respect of the interest free loan in 2020/21 is:**

| £ | Nil |
|---|-----|

No taxable benefit arises if the combined outstanding balance on all loans to the employee did not exceed £10,000 at any time in the tax year.

........................................................................................

## Task 3.17

|  | ✓ |
|-------|---|
| £800 |  |
| £1,295 |  |
| £95 | ✓ |
| £495 |  |

|  | £ |
|---------------------------------------------|-------|
| Annual value | 800 |
| Less contribution (£100 × 12 = £1,200) | (800) |
|  | Nil |

Additional charge

|  | £ | £ |
|------------------------------------------|----------|-------|
| Cost | 97,000 |  |
| Less | (75,000) |  |
| Excess | 22,000 |  |
| £22,000 × 2.25% |  | 495 |
| Less contribution (£1,200 – £800) |  | (400) |
| Total benefit 2020/21 |  | 95 |

The answer £800 is the annual value of the flat. The answer £1,295 ignores the contribution made by Jon. The answer £495 is the additional charge before adjusting for contribution made.

## Task 3.18

| | ✓ |
|---|---|
| Taxable benefit of £700 | |
| Allowable expense of £700 | ✓ |
| Allowable expense of £1,300 | |
| Taxable benefit of £4,550 | |

| | £ | £ |
|---|---|---|
| Amount received 13,000 × 35p | | 4,550 |
| Less statutory amounts | | |
| 10,000 × 45p | 4,500 | |
| 3,000 × 25p | 750 | |
| | | (5,250) |
| Allowable expense | | (700) |

The answer taxable benefit of £700 treats the difference the wrong way round. The answer allowable expense of £1,300 calculates the statutory amounts all at 45p. The answer taxable benefit of £4,550 treats the entire receipt as a benefit.

## Task 3.19

| Item | Taxable | Exempt |
|---|:---:|:---:|
| Interest on loan of £2,000 (only loan provided) | | ✓ |
| Removal costs of £6,000 | | ✓ |
| Use of pool car | | ✓ |
| Reimbursement of business expenses | | ✓ |
| One staff party costing £100 per head | | ✓ |
| Accommodation provided to employee who is not required to live in it for the performance of employment | ✓ | |
| Provision of parking space at work | | ✓ |
| Additional costs of home-working of £6 per week | | ✓ |
| Non-cash long service award of £800 for 22 years of service | | ✓ |
| Accommodation provided to a caretaker for proper performance of his employment duties | | ✓ |
| Work related training | | ✓ |
| Provision of second mobile phone | ✓ | |

## Task 3.20

| | £ |
|---|---:|
| Salary | 30,000 |
| Less    allowable expenses: | |
|     reimbursed expenses | 0 |
|     pension contribution | (2,400) |
|     professional body membership | (150) |
|     fitness club membership | 0 |
|     charitable donation | (600) |
|     clothing | 0 |
|     Mobile telephone (exempt) | 0 |
| Employment income 2020/21 | 26,850 |

## Task 3.21

The maximum amount of relocation expenses that his employer can pay without a taxable benefit arising is:

| £ | 8,000 |
|---|-------|

---

## Task 3.22

| | ✓ |
|---------|---|
| £3,600 | |
| £20,000 | ✓ |
| £26,300 | |
| £24,300 | |

The maximum contribution is the higher of £3,600 and his earnings of £20,000.

Dividends are not earnings.

The answer £3,600 is the statutory maximum contribution without earnings. The answer £26,300 treats dividend income as earnings. The answer £24,300 treats taxable dividend income as earnings.

---

## Task 3.23

Zara's qualifying travel expenses for 2020/21 are:

| £ | 2,100 |
|---|-------|

£300 + £1,800. Travel expenses from home to a permanent workplace are not allowable.

---

## Task 3.24

| | ✓ |
|---|---|
| The employer deducts the contribution after calculating income tax under PAYE. | |
| The employer deducts basic rate tax from the contribution and the employee gets higher rate relief by extending the basic rate band in the tax computation. | |
| The employer deducts the contribution before calculating income tax under PAYE. | ✓ |
| The employer deducts basic rate tax from the contribution and there is no higher rate tax relief. | |

The employer deducts the contribution before calculating income tax, so giving tax relief at the applicable rate/s.

## Task 3.25

| | ✓ |
|---|---|
| The donation is paid net of basic rate tax, and higher rate tax relief is obtained by extending the basic rate band. | |
| The donation is deducted from employment income as an allowable expense before tax is calculated under PAYE. | ✓ |

## Task 3.26

**From:** AATStudent@boxmail.net
**To:** MartinWilkes@boxmail.net
**Sent:** 14 March 2021 12:29
**Subject:** Car

The car benefit is calculated as a percentage of the car's list price, not the actual price paid by the employer.

The percentage (that is multiplied by the list price) is dependent on the car's $CO_2$ emissions rating. For cars which emit $CO_2$ of 55g – 59/km the percentage is 14%, and then this percentage increases by 1% for every additional whole 5g/km of $CO_2$ emissions above 55g/km, up to a maximum of 37%.

In this case, the percentage would be 14% + 17% = 31%.

The percentage is further increased by 4% for a diesel car, unless the car meets RDE2 standards for emissions – has this car got a petrol or a diesel engine?

As the employer will be paying for fuel used for private motoring, a fuel benefit arises. The benefit is a percentage of £24,500. The percentage is the same percentage as is used to calculate the car benefit, ie 31% in this instance.

No benefit arises if you reimburse the whole of the expense of any fuel provided for private use, but there is no reduction to the benefit if only part of the expense for private use fuel is reimbursed, as here. It would be better for the contribution to be set against the use of the car, as this would be deductible in calculating the car benefit.

# Chapter 4

## Task 4.1

Simran's property income for 2020/21 is:

| | ✓ |
|---|---|
| £2,630 | |
| £2,540 | |
| £2,040 | |
| £2,130 | ✓ |

| | £ |
|---|---|
| Rent received (9 months × £500 – accruals basis) | 4,500 |
| Less    electricity | (1,200) |
| water rates | (500) |
| insurance 9/12 × £360 | (270) |
| replacement furniture relief | (400) |
| Property income 2020/21 | 2,130 |

The answer £2,630 includes the rent received on 1 April which is not-taxable under the accruals basis. The answer £2,540 is the cash basis. The answer £2,040 does not pro-rate insurance expenses ie uses cash basis.

## Task 4.2

The amount of taxable property income Julie has for 2020/21 is:

£ | 8,720

| | £ |
|---|---|
| Rent received (cash basis) | 6,300 |
| Less expenses | (660) |
| Replacement furniture relief | (420) |
| Garage | 3,500 |
| Property income 2020/21 | 8,720 |

## Task 4.3

Zelda's property income for 2020/21 is:

| £ | 4,500 |
|---|-------|

| | £ |
|---|---|
| *2018/19* | |
| Income | 6,000 |
| Expenses | (10,000) |
| Loss cfwd | (4,000) |
| | |
| *2019/20* | |
| Income | 8,000 |
| Expenses | (5,500) |
| | 2,500 |
| Less loss b/f | (2,500) |
| | Nil |
| Loss cfwd £1,500 (£4,000 – £2,500) | |
| | |
| *2020/21* | |
| Income | 10,000 |
| Expenses | (4,000) |
| | 6,000 |
| Less loss b/f | (1,500) |
| Taxable property income 2020/21 | 4,500 |

## Task 4.4

Nitin's property income for 2020/21 is:

£ | 12,904

| | £ |
|---|---|
| Rent (£3,600 × 3) | 10,800 |
| Rent (£4,000 × 1) | 4,000 |
| | 14,800 |
| Less   water rates | (195) |
| insurance (£480 × 6/12) | (240) |
| initial repairs: capital | 0 |
| replacement furniture relief | (1,461) |
| Property income 2020/21 | 12,904 |

............................................................

## Task 4.5

Sinead's property income for 2020/21 is:

£ | 7,050

| | £ |
|---|---|
| Property one: rent (4 × £2,000) | 8,000 |
| Property two: rent (5 × £450) | 2,250 |
| Less   expenses on property one | (1,200) |
| expenses on property two | (2,000) |
| Property income 2020/21 | 7,050 |

............................................................

## Task 4.6

| | ✓ |
|---|---|
| Setting the loss of £(5,000) against her employment income in 2020/21 | |
| Carrying forward the loss of £(5,000) against property income in 2021/22 | |
| Setting the loss of £(5,000) first against the profit of £3,000 in 2020/21 and then carrying forward the balance of £(2,000) against property income in 2021/22 | ✓ |
| Setting the loss of £(5,000) first against the profit of £3,000 in 2020/21 and then setting the balance of £(2,000) against employment income in 2020/21 | |

## Task 4.7

| £ | 2,550 |
|---|---|

| | £ |
|---|---|
| Rent (£500 × 12) | 6,000 |
| Rates and insurance (£400 + £250) | (650) |
| Roof repairs | (3,200) |
| Electricity and gas | (1,200) |
| Property income 2020/21 | 950 |

The television is not a deductible expense and does not qualify for replacement furniture relief.

## Task 4.8

**(a)**

|  | ✓ |
| --- | --- |
| Non-savings income | ✓ |
| Savings income |  |
| Dividend income |  |
| Not taxable |  |

**(b)**

|  | ✓ |
| --- | --- |
| 20/40/45% | ✓ |
| 10/20/40/45% |  |
| 0/7.5/32.5/38.1% |  |
| 0/20/40/45% |  |

# Chapter 5

## Task 5.1

| | Class 1 Employee | Class 1 Employer | Class 1A | None |
|---|:---:|:---:|:---:|:---:|
| Salary | ✓ | ✓ | | |
| Company car | | | ✓ | |
| Mileage expenses paid at 35p per mile | | | | ✓ |
| Bonus | ✓ | ✓ | | |
| Department store vouchers | ✓ | ✓ | | |
| Reimbursed travel expenses | | | | ✓ |
| Private gym membership | | | ✓ | |

......................................................................

## Task 5.2

**(a)** **Class 1 Employee**

| £ | 2,332 |
|---|---|

**(b)** **Class 1 Employer**

| £ | 2,789 |
|---|---|

**(c)** **Class 1A**

| £ | 414 |
|---|---|

**Workings**

£27,000/12 months = £2,250 per month.

| Employee | | £ |
|---|:---:|---:|
| £(2,250 – 792) = 1,458 × 12% × 11 months | = | 1,925 |
| £(4,167 – 792) = 3,375 × 12% × 1 month | = | 405 |
| £(2,250 + £2,000 – 4,167) = 83 × 2% × 1 month | = | 2 |
| | = | 2,332 |

| Employer | | £ |
|---|---|---|
| £(2,250 – 732) = 1,518 × 13.8% × 11 months | = | 2,304 |
| £(2,250 + 2,000 – 732) = 3,518 × 13.8% × 1 month | = | 485 |
| | = | 2,789 |
| 1A | | |
| £3,000 × 13.8% | = | 414 |

## Task 5.3

Ann and her employer would be liable to **Class 1 Employee and Employer** on **£45,000** and **Class 1A** on **£300**.

## Task 5.4

| | ✓ |
|---|---|
| True | |
| False | ✓ |

False: this is above the statutory maximum of 45p per mile and so Class 1 Employee and Employer would be payable on the excess.

## Task 5.5

| | ✓ |
|---|---|
| True | |
| False | ✓ |

False: vouchers are deemed to be cash equivalents and so Class 1 Employee and Employer contributions would be due on the cash amount of the vouchers.

## Task 5.6

| | ✓ |
|---|---|
| £nil | |
| £5,106 | |
| £3,893 | ✓ |
| £3,795 | |

**Working**

£(37,000 − 8,788) × 13.8% = £3,893. The employment allowance is not available as Freya is the sole employed earner and a director of Wise Ltd.

The answer £nil deducts the employment allowance. The answer £5,106 ignores the employer threshold. The answer £3,795 uses the employee threshold instead of the employer threshold.

## Task 5.7

**What national insurance contributions are payable by employers and employees on a company car benefit? Please choose from the picklist below:**

| | |
|---|---|
| Employers | Class 1A |
| Employees | None |

Employees do not pay national insurance on benefits.

# Chapter 6

## Task 6.1

For the gain on the disposal of a capital asset to be a chargeable gain there must be a chargeable

| disposal |
|----------|

of a chargeable

| asset |
|-------|

by a chargeable

| person |
|--------|

## Task 6.2

| Item | Chargeable asset | Exempt asset |
|------|:---:|:---:|
| Car | | ✓ |
| A plot of land | ✓ | |
| Jewellery | ✓ | |
| Premium bonds | | ✓ |
| Government stock ('gilts') | | ✓ |

## Task 6.3

| | ✓ |
|------|:---:|
| The gift of an asset | |
| The sale of part of an asset | |
| The transfer of an asset on death | ✓ |
| The sale of the whole of an asset | |

## Task 6.4

| | ✓ |
|---|---|
| £32,800 | ✓ |
| £37,800 | |
| £45,100 | |
| £50,100 | |

| | £ |
|---|---|
| Proceeds of sale | 90,100 |
| Less cost | (40,000) |
| Less enhancement expenditure | (5,000) |
| Chargeable gain | 45,100 |
| Less annual exempt amount | (12,300) |
| Taxable gain | 32,800 |

The answer £37,800 does not deduct the enhancement expenditure. The answer £45,100 does not deduct the annual exempt amount. The answer £50,100 does not deduct the enhancement expenditure or the annual exempt amount.

## Task 6.5

(a) **Lenny's capital gains tax liability for 2020/21 is:**

£ | 908

| | £ |
|---|---|
| Chargeable gains | 20,400 |
| Less allowable losses | (3,560) |
| Net chargeable gains | 16,840 |
| Less annual exempt amount | (12,300) |
| Taxable gains | 4,540 |
| CGT: 4,540 × 20% | 908 |

**(b)** **Lenny's capital gains tax liability is payable by:**

31/01/2022

## Task 6.6

**Larry's capital gains tax liability for 2020/21 is:**

£ 1,180

|  | £ |
|---|---|
| Chargeable gains | 25,400 |
| Less allowable losses | (5,200) |
| Net chargeable gains | 20,200 |
| Less annual exempt amount | (12,300) |
| Taxable gains | 7,900 |

CGT payable

|  | £ |
|---|---|
| £4,000 × 10% | 400 |
| £3,900 × 20% | 780 |
|  | 1,180 |

## Task 6.7

**Laura's capital gains tax liability for 2020/21 is:**

£ 1,214

|  | £ |
|---|---|
| Chargeable gains (£5,400 + £17,500) | 22,900 |
| Less allowable losses | (2,000) |
| Net chargeable gains | 20,900 |
| Less annual exempt amount | (12,300) |
| Taxable gains | 8,600 |

CGT payable

|  | £ |
|---|---|
| £5,065 (W) × 10% | 507 |
| £3,535 × 20% | 707 |
|  | 1,214 |
| (W) Unused basic rate band is £37,500 – £32,435 = £5,065 | |

........................................................................................

## Task 6.8

**Lisa's capital gains tax liability for 2020/21 is:**

| £ | 2,544 |
|---|---|

|  | £ |
|---|---|
| Chargeable gains | 28,000 |
| Less annual exempt amount | (12,300) |
| Taxable gains | 15,700 |
| CGT | |
| £5,965 (W) × 10% | 597 |
| £9,735 × 20% | 1,947 |
|  | 2,544 |
| (W) Unused basic rate band is £37,500 – £31,535 = £5,965 | |

........................................................................................

## Task 6.9

**(a)** **The cost of the land sold is:**

£ | 120,000

$$\frac{240,000}{240,000 + 60,000} \times £150,000$$

**(b)** **The chargeable gain on sale is:**

£ | 117,000

|  | £ |
|---|---|
| Disposal proceeds | 240,000 |
| Less disposal costs | (3,000) |
| Net proceeds | 237,000 |
| Less cost | (120,000) |
| Chargeable gain | 117,000 |

## Task 6.10

|  | ✓ |
|---|---|
| The full amount will be paid on 31 January 2022 | ✓ |
| The full amount will be paid on 31 January 2021 |  |
| Payments on account will be made on 31 January and 31 July 2021, with the balance being paid on 31 January 2022 |  |
| Payments on account will be made on 31 January and 31 July 2020, with the balance being paid on 31 January 2021 |  |

## Task 6.11

**The losses to carry forward to 2021/22 are:**

| £ | 4,200 |
|---|-------|

|  | £ |
|---|---|
| Gains | 20,100 |
| Losses | (7,000) |
|  | 13,100 |
| Less annual exempt amount | (12,300) |
|  | 800 |
| Losses b/f | (800) |
| Taxable gains | Nil |

Losses c/f £(5,000 – 800) = £4,200

## Task 6.12

**Mike's chargeable gain on sale is:**

| £ | 7,000 |
|---|-------|

|  | £ |
|---|---|
| Proceeds of sale | 16,000 |
| Less allowable cost (value at death) | (9,000) |
| Chargeable gain | 7,000 |

## Task 6.13

**Luke's chargeable gain on sale is:**

£ | 17,000

| | £ |
| --- | --- |
| Proceeds of sale | 25,000 |
| Less disposal costs | (2,500) |
| Net proceeds of sale | 22,500 |
| Less allowable cost | |
| 25,000/(25,000 + 50,000) × £(15,000 + 1,500) | (5,500) |
| Chargeable gain | 17,000 |

## Task 6.14

| | ✓ |
| --- | --- |
| True | ✓ |
| False | |

If an individual has allowable losses brought forward, these are allocated after the deduction of the annual exemption and can bring the taxable gain down to nil.

## Task 6.15

**The maximum allowable loss carried forward to 2021/22 will be:**

£ | 12,000

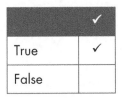

| Tax year | 2018/19 £ | 2019/20 £ | 2020/21 £ |
|---|---|---|---|
| Gains | 2,000 | 4,000 | 14,000 |
| Losses | (14,000) | (2,000)d | (2,000) |
| Net gain/(loss) | (12,000) | 2,000 | 12,000 |
| Less annual exempt amount | (0) | (2,000) | (12,000) |
| Less loss b/f | 0 | 0 | 0 |
| Chargeable gain | 0 | 0 | 0 |
| | | | |
| Loss c/f | (12,000) | (12,000) | (12,000) |

The loss b/f to 2019/20 and 2020/21 was not used as all the gains were covered by the annual exemption.

························································································

## Task 6.16

| | ✓ |
|---|---|
| Beatrice | |
| Susan | |
| Simon | |
| Sarah | ✓ |

Mary is connected to her daughter (Beatrice), her sister-in-law (Susan) and her brother-in-law (Simon). Mary is not connected to her niece (Sarah).

························································································

## Task 6.17

| | ✓ |
|---|---|
| True | |
| False | ✓ |

The loss of £(3,000) can only be set against gains on disposals made to the son (ie the same connected person) in the same tax year or future tax years.

························································································

## Task 6.18

**Her chargeable gain on sale is:**

£ | 833

| | £ |
|---|---|
| Gross proceeds | 6,500 |
| Less costs of sale | (130) |
| Net proceeds | 6,370 |
| Less cost | (1,500) |
| Chargeable gain | 4,870 |
| Gain cannot exceed 5/3 × £(6,500 – 6,000) | 833 |

## Task 6.19

**Jolyon's allowable loss is:**

£ | 1,125

| | £ |
|---|---|
| Deemed proceeds | 6,000 |
| Less costs of sale | (125) |
| Net proceeds | 5,875 |
| Less cost | (7,000) |
| Allowable loss | (1,125) |

## Task 6.20

| | ✓ |
|---|---|
| True | |
| False | ✓ |

Both the proceeds and the cost are less than £6,000 so the gain is exempt.

## Task 6.21

Tick to show the chargeable gain on sale of the picture.

|  | ✓ |
|---|---|
| £1,200 |  |
| £2,200 |  |
| £2,500 | ✓ |
| £3,700 |  |

|  | £ |
|---|---|
| Gross proceeds | 7,500 |
| Less costs of sale | (300) |
| Net proceeds | 7,200 |
| Less cost | (3,500) |
| Chargeable gain | 3,700 |
| Gain cannot exceed 5/3 × £(7,500 – 6,000) | 2,500 |

The answer £1,200 uses a deemed cost of £6,000. The answer £2,200 uses deemed proceeds of £6,000. The answer £3,700 does not make any chattel adjustments.

........................................................

## Task 6.22

Mark's allowable loss is:

| £ | (3,500) |
|---|---|

|  | £ |
|---|---|
| Deemed proceeds | 6,000 |
| Less costs of sale | (500) |
| Net proceeds | 5,500 |
| Less cost | (9,000) |
| Allowable loss | (3,500) |

........................................................

# Chapter 7

## Task 7.1

|  | ✓ |
|---|---|
| Against 10,000 of the shares purchased on 10 May 2008 |  |
| Against 5,000 of the shares purchased on 24 January 2021 and then against 5,000 of the shares purchased on 10 May 2008 |  |
| Against 10,000 of the total shareholding of 20,000 shares |  |
| Against the 8,000 shares purchased on 24 January 2021 and then against 2,000 of the shares purchased on 10 May 2008 | ✓ |

## Task 7.2

**His net chargeable gain on sale is:**

| £ | 9,800 |
|---|---|

Mr Stevens will match his disposal of 5,000 shares on 10 August 2020 to acquisitions as follows:

(1)    1,000 shares bought on 16 August 2020 (next 30 days, FIFO basis)

(2)    4,000 shares from the share pool (which only consists of the 6,000 shares bought in July 2018)

Disposal of 1,000 shares bought on 16 August 2020

|  | £ |
|---|---|
| Proceeds of sale £20,000 × 1,000/5,000 | 4,000 |
| Less cost | (4,200) |
| Allowable loss | (200) |

Disposal of 4,000 shares bought from the share pool (= July 2018 acquisition)

| | £ |
|---|---|
| Proceeds of sale £20,000 × 4,000/5,000 | 16,000 |
| Less cost £9,000 × 4,000/6,000 | (6,000) |
| Chargeable gain | 10,000 |
| | |
| Net chargeable gain = £10,000 – 200 | 9,800 |

## Task 7.3

### Share pool

| | No. of shares | Cost £ |
|---|---|---|
| 10 February 2001 | 12,000 | 18,000 |
| 20 September 2008 Bonus 1:4 (1/4 × 12,000 = 3,000 shares) | 3,000 | 0 |
| | 15,000 | 18,000 |
| 15 March 2021 Disposal (£18,000 × 2,000/15,000 = £2,400) | (2,000) | (2,400) |
| | 13,000 | 15,600 |

### Gain on sale

| | £ |
|---|---|
| Proceeds | 8,000 |
| Less cost | (2,400) |
| Gain | 5,600 |

## Task 7.4

Mark will match his disposal of 10,000 shares on 4 November 2020 as follows:

(1) 2,000 shares bought on 10 November 2020
(2) 8,000 shares from share pool

|  | £ |
|---|---|
| Disposal of 2,000 shares bought on 10 November 2020: | |
| Proceeds $\dfrac{2,000}{10,000} \times £60,000$ | 12,000 |
| Less cost | (11,500) |
| Chargeable gain | 500 |
| Disposal of 8,000 shares from share pool: | |
| Proceeds $\dfrac{8,000}{10,000} \times £60,000$ | 48,000 |
| Less cost (W) | (12,200) |
| Chargeable gain | 35,800 |
| | |
| Total chargeable gain (£500 + £35,800) | 36,300 |

| Share pool working | No. of shares | Cost £ |
|---|---|---|
| 9 December 2001 | 12,000 | 4,400 |
| 12 October 2005 Rights 1:3 × £5 | 4,000 | 20,000 |
| (1/3 × 12,000 = 4,000 shares × £5 = £20,000) | | |
| | 16,000 | 24,400 |
| 4 November 2020 Disposal | (8,000) | (12,200) |
| (£24,400 × 8,000/16,000 = £12,200) | | |
| | 8,000 | 12,200 |

## Task 7.5

|  | £ |
|---|---|
| Disposal proceeds | 3,675,000 |
| Less cost (W) | (537,600) |
| Chargeable gain | 3,137,400 |

**Working: share pool**

|  | Number | Cost £ |
|---|---|---|
| Purchase June 2006 | 500,000 | 960,000 |
| Bonus issue December 2011 |  |  |
| 500,000 × 3/2 | 750,000 | 0 |
| Disposal September 2020 | 1,250,000 | 960,000 |
| 960,000 × 700,000/1,250,000 | (700,000) | (537,600) |
| Balance carried forward | 550,000 | 422,400 |

# Chapter 8

## Task 8.1

|  | ✓ |
|---|---|
| 16.5/25 | ✓ |
| 10.75/25 | |
| 15.75/25 | |
| 8.5/25 | |

|  | Chargeable | Exempt |
|---|---|---|
| Actual occupation | | 8.75 |
| Employment abroad (actual occupation before and after period of absence) – any period | | 5 |
| Actual occupation | | 2 |
| Absence (not followed by period of actual occupation) | 8.5 | |
| Last nine months of ownership | | 0.75 |
| Totals | 8.5 | 16.5 |

The answer 10.75/25 is periods of actual occupation only. The answer 15.75/25 ignores the last nine months deemed residence. The answer 8.5/25 is the chargeable fraction.

## Task 8.2

|  | ✓ |
|---|---|
| True | ✓ |
| False | |

The period when the property was unoccupied will be covered by the last nine months deemed occupation rule.

## Task 8.3

| | £ |
|---|---|
| Proceeds | 180,000 |
| Less cost | (50,000) |
| Gain before private residence exemption | 130,000 |
| Less private residence exemption | (63,289) |
| Chargeable gain | 66,711 |

**Working**

| | Exempt years | Chargeable years |
|---|---|---|
| 1.8.01 – 31.7.04 (actual occupation) | 3 | |
| 1.8.04 – 31.7.08 (up to 4 years due to place of work not employed abroad) | 4 | |
| 1.8.08 – 31.7.09 (up to 3 years any reason) | 1 | |
| 1.8.09 – 31.1.10 (actual occupation) | 0.5 | |
| 1.2.10 – 20.10.19 (not followed by actual occupation) | | 9.75 |
| 1.11.19 – 31.7.20 (last nine months) | 0.75 | |
| Totals | 9.25 | 9.75 |

## Task 8.4

| | ✓ |
|---|---|
| 13.75/14.5 | ✓ |
| 13.5/14.5 | |
| 10.5/14.5 | |
| 10.75/14.5 | |

| | Exempt years | Chargeable years | Total years |
|---|---|---|---|
| Actual occupation | 3 | | 3 |
| Deemed occupation – any time employed overseas | 5 | | 5 |
| Actual occupation | 2 | | 2 |
| Deemed occupation – up to 3 years any reason | 3 | | 3 |
| Unoccupied | | 0.75 | 0.75 |
| Last nine months of ownership | 0.75 | | 0.75 |
| Totals | 13.75 | 0.75 | 14.5 |

The answer 13.5/14.5 ignores the final nine months of deemed ownership. The answer 10.5/14.5 ignores deemed occupation for three years for any reason and the final nine months. The answer 10.75 ignore the deemed occupation for three years for any reason eg forgets Jose returned to the house for the final six months.

········································································

## Task 8.5

| | ✓ |
|---|---|
| True | |
| False | ✓ |

Periods of time working abroad are only covered by the deemed occupation rules if the owner lives in the property before and after the absence.

········································································

# Chapter 9

### Task 9.1

| | PET | CLT | Exempt |
|---|---|---|---|
| Gift of £100 cash to niece | | | ✓<br>small gift |
| Gift of shares to a trust | | ✓ | |
| Payment of grandson's school fees out of income surplus to living requirements | | | ✓<br>Payment out of income – does not reduce standard of living |
| Gift of £5,000 to son on the occasion of his marriage | | | ✓ |
| Gift of £25,000 to friend | ✓ | | |
| Gift of classic car to spouse | | | ✓<br>Transfers between spouses/civil partners are exempt |
| Gift of £10,000 to a trust | | ✓ | |

### Task 9.2

| £ | 550,000 |
|---|---|

Norman's nil band at death was £325,000 with £100,000 being used on the transfer to his cousin. The remaining £225,000 is added to the nil band of Maureen of £325,000 making a total nil band of £550,000 available to Maureen on her death.

## Task 9.3

|  | Deductible ✓ | Not deductible ✓ |
|---|---|---|
| Grocery bill | ✓ | |
| HM Revenue & Customs – income tax to death | ✓ | |
| Mortgage on home | ✓ | |
| Illegal gambling debt | | ✓ |

Grocery bill – deductible as incurred for consideration

Income tax to death – deductible as imposed by law

Mortgage – deductible, will be set against value of house primarily

Illegal gambling debt – not deductible as not legally enforceable

## Task 9.4

|  | ✓ |
|---|---|
| True | |
| False | ✓ |

A PET is only subject to Inheritance Tax on the death of the donor if the death occurs within seven years of the gift

## Task 9.5

|  | ✓ |
|---|---|
| True | |
| False | ✓ |

The £5,000 exemption only applies to gifts on marriage from parent to child.

## Task 9.6

| Lifetime tax | Death tax | ✓ |
|---|---|---|
| 31 January 2021 | 30 June 2021 | |
| 30 April 2021 | 30 June 2021 | ✓ |
| 31 January 2021 | 30 April 2021 | |
| 30 April 2021 | 30 April 2021 | |

Lifetime tax 30 April 2021, death tax 30 June 2021

For chargeable lifetime transfers the due date is the later of 30 April just after the end of the tax year of the transfer and six months after the end of the month of the transfer. The due date for the tax arising on death is six months from the end of the month of death.

······························································································

## Task 9.7

| | ✓ |
|---|---|
| £87,250 | ✓ |
| £69,800 | |
| £88,750 | |
| £22,250 | |

**Workings**

| | £ |
|---|---|
| Gift | 420,000 |
| Less AEs 2020/21, 2019/20 b/f | (6,000) |
| Net chargeable transfer | 414,000 |
| Less nil band remaining £(325,000 – 260,000) | (65,000) |
| | 349,000 |
| IHT @ 20/80 | 87,250 |

The gross chargeable transfer in August 2016 is after any exemptions but the gift in November 2020 must have the annual exemptions deducted to find the net chargeable transfer.

The answer £69,800 calculates IHT at 20% ie assumes trustees pay. The answer £88,750 does not deduct the annual exemptions from the gift. The answer £22,250 does not adjust the nil rate band for the previous CLT.

## Task 9.8

| 257.5 | p |
|-------|---|

**Workings**

lower of:

$\frac{1}{4}$ up: $\frac{280 - 250}{4} + 250 = 257.5$

Average: $\frac{279 + 252}{2} = 265.5$

## Task 9.9

| £ | 2,750 |
|---|-------|

**Workings**

|  | £ |
|---|---|
| Before transfer: 500 shares at £10 | 5,000 |
| After transfer: 300 shares at £7.50 | 2,250 |
| Transfer of value | 2,750 |

## Task 9.10

|  | ✓ |
|---|---|
| £340,000 |  |
| £210,000 | ✓ |
| £280,000 |  |
| £290,000 |  |

**Workings**

| | £ |
|---|---|
| Estate | 1,225,000 |
| Less Exempt legacy to husband | (200,000) |
| | 1,025,000 |
| Less residence nil rate band 2020/21 | (175,000) |
| Less nil band 2020/21 | (325,000) |
| | 525,000 |
| IHT @ 40% | 210,000 |

The answer £340,000 assumes to nil rate band. The answer £280,000 assumes no residence nil rate band. The answer £290,000 ignores the exempt legacy to her husband.

## *Chapter 10*

### Task 10.1

The tax year 2020/21 runs from:

| 06/04/2020 |

until:

| 05/04/2021 |

### Task 10.2

| | ✓ |
|---|---|
| True | ✓ |
| False | |

### Task 10.3

**The UK tax system is administered by.**

| | ✓ |
|---|---|
| Parliament | |
| Her Majesty's Revenue & Customs (HMRC) | ✓ |
| National Crime Agency (NCA) | |
| HM Customs & Excise | |

### Task 10.4

| | ✓ |
|---|---|
| HMRC | |
| Your firm's Money Laundering Reporting Officer | ✓ |
| National Crime Agency | |
| Tax Tribunal | |

## Task 10.5

Please be assured that an ethical guideline of confidentiality applies in your dealings with our firm.

This guideline means that your personal information will remain confidential, unless you give us authority to disclose information to third parties such as members of your family.

## Task 10.6

|  | ✓ |
|---|---|
| If the client is unwell and unable to respond to HMRC |  |
| If money laundering is suspected | ✓ |
| Where it would be illegal not to disclose the information | ✓ |
| If the information is requested from a 'connected person' |  |

## Task 10.7

The five fundamental principles of professional ethics for AAT members are:

| I | Integrity |
|---|---|
| O | Objectivity |
| Pc and dc | Professional competence and due care |
| C | Confidentiality |
| Pb | Professional behaviour |

## Task 10.8

|  | ✓ |
|---|---|
| HMRC |  |
| Another firm's Money Laundering Reporting Officer |  |
| National Crime Agency | ✓ |
| Tax Tribunal |  |

## Task 10.9

| | ✓ |
| --- | --- |
| True | |
| False | ✓ |

A non-UK resident individual is only liable to pay income tax on their UK income.

## Task 10.10

You should inform the client that this represents theft and they should tell HMRC of their mistake immediately.

If they refuse to tell HMRC then you will need to warn them of the consequences of not informing HMRC of their mistake. If HMRC do discover this error, then there would be interest and penalties (criminal and civil) due as well as the expectation that the initial amount of the refund would need to be repaid.

If they still refuse, then you should cease to act for the client and inform HMRC that you have ceased to act for them. You cannot tell HMRC why you are ceasing to act for the client as this would be a breach of confidentiality.

You have a professional responsibility to neither break the law nor assist others to do so.

Ensure all correspondence is in writing and saved in the file.

## Task 10.11

| | ✓ |
| --- | --- |
| True | |
| False | ✓ |

Tax avoidance is the use of tax legislation in a way that was not intended to reduce tax liabilities. It is legal but can be considered unethical.

Tax evasion is illegal.

# AAT AQ2016 ASSESSMENT 1
## Personal Tax

## Time allowed: 2.5 hours

*You are advised to attempt the AAT practice/sample assessment 1 online from the AAT website. This will ensure you are prepared for how the assessment will be presented on the AAT's system when you attempt the real assessment. Please access the assessment using the address below:*

*https://www.aat.org.uk/training/study-support/search*

**AAT AQ2016 PRACTICE ASSESSMENT**

# AAT AQ2016 ASSESSMENT 2
## Personal Tax

*You are advised to attempt sample assessment 2 online from the AAT website. This will ensure you are prepared for how the assessment will be presented on the AAT's system when you attempt the real assessment. Please access the assessment using the address below:*

https://www.aat.org.uk/training/study-support/search

# BPP PRACTICE ASSESSMENT 1
# PERSONAL TAX

**Time allowed: 2.5 hours**

# Personal Tax (PLTX)
# BPP practice assessment 1

In the live assessment you will have access to the tax tables and reference material which have been reproduced at the back of this Question Bank. Please use them while completing this practice assessment so that you are familiar with their content.

## Task 1 (10 marks)

You work for a firm of accountants. A few weeks ago, you prepared a tax return for Sharon. Sharon has now told you that she forgot to include some bank interest in the return but that she does not intend to tell HM Revenue & Customs (HMRC) of the omission.

**Explain what steps you should take regarding this information.**

## Task 2 (8 marks)

Shane is provided with a company car for business and private use throughout 2020/21. The car had a list price of £16,700 when bought new in December 2018, although the company paid £15,000 for the car after a dealer discount. It has a petrol engine, with $CO_2$ emissions of 93g/km. The company pays for all running costs, including all fuel. Shane does not make any contribution for his private use of the car.

**(a)** Complete the following sentences: **(6 marks)**

**The cost of the car in the taxable benefit computation is:**

£ [                    ]

**The percentage used in the taxable benefit computation is:**

[                    ] %

The taxable benefit in respect of the provision of fuel for private use is:

£ [ ]

The percentage used in the taxable benefit computation if the car is diesel and does not meet the conditions of RDE2 is:

£ [ ]

**(b)** Complete the following table by inserting the scale charge for 2020/21 for each of the cars shown below. **(2 marks)**

| | Engine type | CO₂ emissions | Scale charge % |
|---|---|---|---|
| Car 1 | Diesel (meets the conditions of RDE2 and registered after April 2020) | 131 | |
| Car 2 | Petrol (registered before April 2020) | 152 | |

## Task 3 (8 marks)

**(a)** Josie is a basic rate taxpayer and receives the following benefits as the result of her employment.

**In each case enter the taxable benefit arising in 2020/21. If the benefit is exempt, enter 0.** **(6 marks)**

**(1)** **A mobile telephone for private and business use throughout the year. The purchase of the phone and the calls from it cost her employer a total of £350 for 2020/21.**

£ [ ]

**(2)** **Payment of £50 for incidental overnight expenses whilst staying away in the UK for five nights.**

£ [ ]

**(3)** **Leisure club membership for Josie costing her employer £5,000 using a corporate discount scheme. If a member of the public had taken this membership it would have cost £6,500.**

£ [ ]

(4)   Use of a house near her work that enables her to start work at 7.00am every morning. The house has an annual value of £5,900 and cost her employer £227,000 4 years ago.

£ [          ]

(b)   For each of the following benefits, tick whether they would be wholly or partly taxable or wholly exempt if received in 2020/21:                                    (2 marks)

| Item | Wholly or partly taxable | Wholly exempt |
|---|---|---|
| Interest on loan of £8,000 (only loan provided) | | |
| Additional costs of home working of £7 per week (no evidence presented to employer) | | |
| Use of pool car | | |
| One staff party costing £120 per head | | |

## Task 4 (6 marks)

During 2020/21, Eva received the following income.

**In each case, show the amount of income that she should enter on her tax return. If the income is exempt, enter 0.**

(a)   **Employment income £20,000, tax deducted £2,700.**

£ [          ]

(b)   **Government stock ('gilt') interest £40.**

£ [          ]

(c)   **Interest on ISA account £90.**

£ [          ]

(d)   **Dividends received from a UK company £1,280.**

£ [          ]

## Task 5 (6 marks)

**(a)** Emily lets a furnished house for £150 a week. During 2020/21 the flat was let for 40 weeks. It was unoccupied for the remaining 12 weeks of the year.

During 2020/21, Emily spent £190 on advertising for tenants, £460 on water rates, £800 on redecoration, £690 on electricity and £368 on cleaning. Emily also installed a new central heating system at a cost of £1,200. Previously, the house did not have central heating. Emily replaced some furniture at a cost of £554 during 2020/21.

Emily uses the accruals basis to calculate her property profits.

**Calculate the property income taxable on Emily for 2020/21 using the proforma layout provided. Fill in all the unshaded boxes. If any item is not an allowable expense, enter 0. Both brackets and minus signs can be used to show negative numbers.** **(4 marks)**

|                          | £ |
|--------------------------|---|
| Rent                     |   |
| Expenses:                |   |
| Advertising              |   |
| Water rates              |   |
| Redecoration             |   |
| Electricity              |   |
| Cleaning                 |   |
| Central heating system   |   |
| Furniture cost           |   |
| **Property income**      |   |

**(b)** Oliver owns an investment property in Cornwall, which he uses personally for weekends away and occasionally rents to friends. His rental income received during 2020/21 was £2,500, and his allowable expenses (as apportioned for the let periods) were £900.

**What is Oliver's taxable property profits for 2020/21, assuming he makes any relevant elections?** **(2 marks)**

| | ✓ |
|---|---|
| £1,000 | |
| £1,500 | ╱ |
| £1,600 | |
| £2,500 | |

## Task 6 (12 marks)

**(a)** During 2020/21 Elaine earned £115,000 of employment income and received bank interest of £5,000 and dividends of £18,000.

**Calculate her total income tax liability to the nearest pound for 2020/21, entering your answer and workings in the blank table given below. You have been given more space than you will need.** **(9 marks)**

| | N$_{on}$ | Sav | Div |
|---|---|---|---|
| Salary | 115,000 | | |
| Bank interest | | 5000 | |
| Dividends | | | 18,000 |
| Total | 138,000 | | |
| Less PA | (5000) | | |
| 37,500 × 20% | 7500 | | |
| 100,500 × 40 | 40,200 | | |
| 500 × 0 | | | |
| 4500 × 40% | 1800 | | |
| 18000×0 % | | | |
| 16000 × 38.5% | 5200 | | |

|  |  |  |  |
| --- | --- | --- | --- |
|  |  |  |  |
|  |  |  |  |
|  |  |  |  |
|  |  |  |  |

**(b)** Elaine is a higher rate tax payer and is considering making a Gift Aid donation of £500 each year to a charity. However, she does not understand the tax implications of doing this.

**Explain to Elaine how she will get tax relief on such donations, and the tax implications if she had made a £500 Gift Aid donation during 2020/21.** **(3 marks)**

## Task 7 (4 marks)

Tom has employment income of £75,000 in 2020/21. He is provided with a company car and private fuel throughout the year. The taxable benefit arising from these benefits totals £4,500.

**Complete the following sentences by typing your answer, in whole pounds, in the boxes provided. Ignore the employment allowance.**

The total Class 1 employee's national insurance contributions payable by Tom in 2020/21 are:

£

The total Class 1 employer's national insurance contributions payable by Tom's employer in 2020/21 are:

£ [handwritten]

The total Class 1A national insurance contributions payable by Tom's employer in 2020/21 are:

£ [handwritten]

## Task 8 (7 marks)

A recently retired client has approached your manager about the tax planning opportunities available for inheritance tax.

**Please could you write some notes for your manager's meeting with the client.**

## Task 9 (10 marks)

**(a)** For each of the following assets, tick the relevant column to indicate whether they are chargeable or exempt assets for capital gains tax: **(4 marks)**

| Asset | Chargeable | Exempt |
|---|---|---|
| Car used solely for business purposes | | |
| Holiday cottage | | |
| Vintage car worth £40,000 | | |
| Shares held in an individual savings account | | |

**(b)** Rodney purchased an antique chair for £1,450. On 10 October 2020 he sold the chair at auction for £6,300 (which was net of the auctioneer's 10% commission).

**The chargeable gain on sale is:** **(2 marks)**

£

**(c)** Andrew bought six acres of land for £405,000. He sold two acres of the land at auction for £360,000. His disposal costs were £6,000. The market value of the four remaining acres at the date of sale was £540,000.

**Complete the following sentences.** **(4 marks)**

**(1)** The cost of the land sold is:

£

**(2)** The chargeable gain on sale is:

£

## Task 10 (10 marks)

In August 2010 Wayne acquired 4,000 shares in Main plc at a cost of £10,000. In September 2012, there was a one for one bonus issue when the shares were worth £8 each. Wayne sold 3,000 shares in July 2013 for £15,000 and purchased 3,000 back again in October 2013 for £12,000.

Wayne sold half of his shareholding in June 2020 for £21,000.

**Clearly showing the balance of shares and their value to carry forward, calculate the gain made on the sale of the shares in 2020/21. All workings must be shown in your calculations.**

| | | |
|---|---|---|
| August 2010 | 4000 | 10,000 |
| Sep 2012   1 for 1 Bonus | 4000 | — |
| 30 | 8000 | 10,000 |
| July 2013 Sale (3/8 × 10,000) | (3000) | (3750) |
| | 5000 | 6250 |
| Oct 2013 | 5000 | 12000 |
| | 8000 | 18,250 |
| June 2020 ( | (4000) | (9,125) |
| | 4000 | 9125 |
| | | |
| Proceeds | 21,000 | |
| Cost (Pool) | (9,125) | |
| Gain | 11,875 | |
| | | |
| | | |
| | | |
| | | |

## Task 11 (7 marks)

**(a)** For each of the following statements, tick if they are True or False.

**(2 marks)**

|  | True | False |
|---|---|---|
| Any CGT annual exempt amount that is unused in one tax year can be carried forward to be used in the following tax year only. |  |  |
| Capital losses in a tax year must be offset against capital gains in that year, even if it means losing all, or some of the annual exempt amount. |  |  |

**(b)** Charlotte bought a house on 1 February 2008 for £95,000 and sold it for £263,000 on 1 October 2020. During the period of ownership the following occurred:

| 01.02.08 to 31.10.10 | Charlotte lived in the property ³³ |
|---|---|
| 01.11.10 to 31.03.19 | Charlotte worked elsewhere in the UK |
| 01.04.19 to 30.09.20 | Charlotte lived in the property until she sold it |

**Input the correct answers in the boxes provided to complete the sentences. Where applicable round your answer to the nearest whole number.** **(3 marks)**

The total period of ownership of the property is [          ] months.

The period of Charlotte's actual and deemed residence is [          ] months.

The chargeable gain on the sale of the house is [          ].

144

**(c)** Ella purchased an antique clock for £12,000. She sold it on 1 September 2020 for £63,000. Ella has no other chargeable assets. Her taxable income for 2020/21 was £34,500. Complete the following sentences.

**(2 marks)**

**Ella's CGT payable for 2020/21 is:**

£ 

**This is payable by (xx/xx/xxxx):**



## Task 12 (6 marks)

**(a)** Andy and Hilda had been married for many years when Andy died in June 2011. 60% of Andy's nil rate band was unused on his death. The nil rate band at Andy's death was £325,000. Hilda died in December 2020. Her only lifetime transfers of value were cash gifts of £6,000 to her nephew in January 2020 and £10,000 to her niece in March 2020. Hilda did not own any property on her death.

**What is the maximum nil rate band available for use against Hilda's death estate?** **(3 marks)**

£ 

**(b)** **For each of the following statements, tick if they are true or false.** **(3 marks)**

| | True | False |
|---|---|---|
| A CLT is only chargeable on death of the donor. | | |
| Cars are exempt from IHT. | | |
| The annual exemption for the current year is used before any unused annual exemption brought forward from the prior year. | | |

## Task 13 (6 marks)

Jessica made a gross chargeable lifetime transfer of £60,000 (after exemptions) in August 2018. In November 2020, she gave £400,000 to a trust for the benefit of her son. Jessica agreed to pay any lifetime IHT due.

**How much inheritance tax will be payable by Jessica on the transfer of value in November 2020?**

# BPP PRACTICE ASSESSMENT 1
# PERSONAL TAX

## ANSWERS

# Personal Tax (PLTX)
## BPP practice assessment 1

### Task 1 (10 marks)

You should inform Sharon of the implications of not reporting this income to HMRC and that it could be viewed as tax evasion which is punishable by fines/imprisonment.

If she refuses to inform HMRC of this income then you should let her know, in writing, that it is not possible for your firm to continue to act for her.

You should then inform HMRC that your firm is no longer acting for Sharon but you should not give details of why you are ceasing to act as this would be a breach of confidentiality.

You should then make a report to your firm's Money Laundering Reporting Officer of Sharon's refusal to disclose the omission to HMRC and the facts surrounding it.

### Task 2 (8 marks)

**(a)**                                                               **(6 marks)**

The cost of the car in the taxable benefit computation is:

| £ | 16,700 |
|---|--------|

The percentage used in the taxable benefit computation is:

| | 23 | % |
|---|---|---|

14% + (90 – 55)/5% + 2% (pre-April 2020)

The taxable benefit in respect of the provision of fuel for private use is:

| £ | 5,635 |
|---|-------|

£24,500 × 23%

The percentage used in the taxable benefit computation if the car was diesel and does not meet the conditions of RDE2 is:

| | 27 | % |
|---|---|---|

23% + 4% diesel supplement

**(b)** Complete the following table by inserting the scale charge for 2020/21 for each of the cars shown below. **(2 marks)**

| | Engine type | CO$_2$ emissions | Scale charge % |
|---|---|---|---|
| Car 1 | Diesel (meets the conditions of RDE2, registered after April 2020) | 131 | 29% |
| Car 2 | Petrol (registered before April 2020) | 152 | 35% |

# Task 3 (8 marks)

**(a)** **(6 marks)**

**(1)** Mobile telephone

| £ | 0 |
|---|---|

**(2)** Overnight expenses

| £ | 50 |
|---|---|

If paid over £5 per night for stays in the UK then the whole amount is taxable.

**(3)** Leisure club membership (cost to employer)

| £ | 5,000 |
|---|---|

**(4)** Home £5,900 + ((£227,000 – 75,000) × 2.25%))

| £ | 9,320 |
|---|---|

**(b)** **(2 marks)**

| Item | Wholly or partly taxable | Wholly exempt |
|---|---|---|
| Interest on loan of £8,000 (only loan provided) | | ✓(£10,000 or less) |
| Additional costs of home working of £7 per week (no evidence presented to employer) | ✓(evidence needed if more than £6 per week) | |
| Use of pool car | | ✓ |
| One staff party costing £120 per head | | ✓(up to £150) |

## Task 4 (6 marks)

**(a)** Employment income £20,000, tax deducted £2,700.

| £ | 20,000 |
|---|--------|

**(b)** Government stock ('gilt') interest £40.

| £ | 40 |
|---|----|

**(c)** Interest on ISA account £90.

| £ | 0 |
|---|---|

Exempt

**(d)** Dividends received £1,280.

| £ | 1,280 |
|---|-------|

## Task 5 (6 marks)

**(a)** **(4 marks)**

|  | £ |
|---|---|
| Rent accrued £150 × 40 | 6,000 |
| Expenses: |  |
| Advertising | (190) |
| Water rates | (460) |
| Redecoration | (800) |
| Electricity | (690) |
| Cleaning | (368) |
| Central heating system (capital) | (0) |
| Furniture cost | (554) |
| **Property income** | 2,938 |

**(b)** **(2 marks)**

| | ✓ |
|---|---|
| £1,000 | |
| £1,500 | ✓ |
| £1,600 | |
| £2,500 | |

£2,500 – £1,000 (property allowance) = £1,500.

Oliver will use the property allowance of £1,000 in preference to his actual expenses, as this gives a lower taxable profit.

The answer £1,000 is the property allowance. The answer £1,600 deducts his actual expenses. The answer £2,500 is the rental income received.

## Task 6 (12 marks)

**(a)** **(9 marks)**

| | Non-savings £ | Interest £ | Dividends £ |
|---|---|---|---|
| Employment Income | 115,000 | | |
| Bank interest | | 5,000 | |
| Dividends | | | 18,000 |
| Net income | 115,000 | 5,000 | 18,000 |
| Personal allowance (net income > £125,000) | (nil) | | |
| Taxable income | 115,000 | 5,000 | 18,000 |
| | | | |
| £37,500 × 20% | 7,500 | | |
| £77,500 (£115,000 – £37,500) × 40% | 31,000 | | |
| £500 × 0% + £4,500 × 40% | 1,800 | | |
| £2,000 × 0% + £16,000 × 32.5% | 5,200 | | |
| Income tax liability | 45,500 | | |

**(b)** **(3 marks)**

> If you make a Gift Aid donation of £500 each year to charity this amount will be grossed up at the basic rate of tax, giving a gross amount received by the charity of £625. Hence you will immediately have 20% relief.
>
> This gross figure of £625 will be used to extend the upper limit of the basic rate band to give an upper limit of £38,125 (£37,500 + £625) and will also extend the additional rate threshold to £150,625 (£150,000 + £625).
>
> This would mean that an extra £625 of your employment income would be taxed at the basic rate of tax of 20% instead of at the higher rate of tax of 40%, thereby giving another 20% relief to give you 40% relief in total.

## Task 7 (4 marks)

The total Class 1 employee's national insurance contributions payable by Tom in 2020/21 are:

| £ | 5,360 |
|---|-------|

(£50,000 – £9,500) × 12% = £4,860

(£75,000 – £50,000) × 2% = £500

The total Class 1 employer's national insurance contributions payable by Tom's employer in 2020/21 are:

| £ | 9,137 |
|---|-------|

(£75,000 – £8,788) × 13.8% = £9,137

The total Class 1A national insurance contributions payable by Tom's employer in 2020/21 are:

| £ | 621 |
|---|-----|

£4,500 × 13.8% = £621

## Task 8 (7 marks)

Inheritance tax planning:

Gift assets during lifetime to make use of available exemptions such as the marriage and annual exemptions.

Gift assets early – gifts, except gifts to trusts, are exempt from IHT if the donor survives for more than seven years from the date of the gift. Should the donor die within seven years but at least three years after the gift then taper relief applies to reduce the amount of tax payable.

Avoid making gifts to trusts in excess of the available nil band, as these generate an immediate charge to IHT.

Use the nil rate band effectively every seven years.

Make use of the spouse/civil partner exemption and transfer assets to the younger spouse so that they can gift them and hopefully they will then be exempt by the seven-year rule.

Gift main homes in death estate rather than during lifetime, to direct descendants, in order to benefit from the residence nil rate band.

## Task 9 (10 marks)

### (a)

(4 marks)

| Asset | Chargeable | Exempt |
|---|---|---|
| Car used solely for business purposes | | ✓ |
| Holiday cottage | ✓ | |
| Vintage car worth £40,000 | | ✓ |
| Shares held in an individual savings account | | ✓ |

### (b)

(2 marks)

The chargeable gain on sale is:

| £ | 1,667 |
|---|---|

|  | £ |
|---|---|
| Disposal proceeds £6,300 × 100/90 | 7,000 |
| Less disposal costs £7,000 × 10% | (700) |
| Net proceeds | 6,300 |
| Less cost | (1,450) |
| Gain | 4,850 |
| Cannot exceed 5/3 × £(7,000 – 6,000) | 1,667 |

**(c)** **(4 marks)**

**(1)** The cost of the land sold is:

£ | 162,000

$$\frac{360,000}{360,000 + 540,000} \times £405,000$$

**(2)** The chargeable gain on sale is:

£ | 192,000

|  | £ |
|---|---|
| Disposal proceeds | 360,000 |
| Less disposal costs | (6,000) |
| Net proceeds | 354,000 |
| Less cost | (162,000) |
| Chargeable gain | 192,000 |

# Task 10 (10 marks)

|  | £ |
|---|---|
| Proceeds of sale | 21,000 |
| Less cost | (9,125) |
| Gain | 11,875 |

|  | No. of shares | Cost £ |
|---|---|---|
| August 2010 Acquisition | 4,000 | 10,000 |
| September 2012 Bonus 1 for 1 | 4,000 | nil |
|  | 8,000 | 10,000 |
| July 2013 Disposal (3,000/8,000 × £10,000) | (3,000) | (3,750) |
|  | 5,000 | 6,250 |
| October 2013 Acquisition | 3,000 | 12,000 |
|  | 8,000 | 18,250 |
| June 2020 Disposal (4,000/8,000 × £18,250) | (4,000) | (9,125) |
| c/f | 4,000 | 9,125 |

## Task 11 (7 marks)

**(a)** (2 marks)

|  | True | False |
|---|---|---|
| Any CGT annual exempt amount that is unused in one tax year can be carried forward to be used in the following tax year only. |  | ✓ |
| Capital losses in a tax year must be offset against capital gains in that year, even if it means losing all, or some of the annual exempt amount. | ✓ |  |

Any unused annual exempt amount is lost.

Only capital losses brought forward can be restricted to ensure the annual exempt amount isn't lost.

**(b)**                                                **(3 marks)**

The total period of ownership of the property is      152      months.

The period of Charlotte's actual and deemed residence is      135      months.

| 01.02.08 to 31.10.10 | 33 months actual occupation |
|---|---|
| 01.11.10 to 31.03.19 | 48 months – deemed occupation – working elsewhere in UK – preceded and followed by actual occupation |
| | 36 months – deemed occupation – any reason – preceded and followed by actual occupation |
| | 17 months non-occupation |
| 01.04.19 to 30.09.20 | 18 months – actual occupation (last nine months always deemed occupation anyway) |

The chargeable gain on the sale of the house is      £18,789      .

| | £ |
|---|---|
| Disposal proceeds | 263,000 |
| Less cost | (95,000) |
| | 168,000 |
| Private residence relief £168,000 × 135/152 | (149,211) |
| Chargeable gain | 18,789 |

**(c)**                                                **(2 marks)**

Ella's CGT payable for 2020/21 is:

£     7,440

This is payable by:

31/01/2022

| | £ |
|---|---|
| Disposal proceeds | 63,000 |
| Less cost | (12,000) |
| Gain | 51,000 |
| Less annual exempt amount | (12,300) |
| Taxable gain | 38,700 |
| | |
| CGT | |
| | |
| On £3,000 × 10% (unused basic rate band £37,500 – £34,500) | 300 |
| On £35,700 × 20% | 7,140 |
| | 7,440 |

## Task 12 (6 marks)

**(a)** (3 marks)

£ | 510,000

| | £ |
|---|---|
| Andy's unused nil band: (60% × £325,000) | 195,000 |
| Hilda's nil band at death (325,000 – 10,000) | 315,000 |
| Total nil band available to Hilda | 510,000 |

The cash gift to Hilda's nephew (a PET) is covered by her annual exemptions (2 × £3,000) so does not use up any of the nil rate band.

**(b)**                                                                    **(3 marks)**

|  | True | False |
|---|---|---|
| A CLT is only chargeable on death of the donor. |  | ✓ |
| Cars are exempt from IHT. |  | ✓ |
| The annual exemption for the current year is used before any unused annual exemption brought forward from the prior year. | ✓ |  |

## Task 13 (6 marks)

|  | £ |
|---|---|
| Gift | 400,000 |
| Less AEs 2020/21, 2019/20 b/f | (6,000) |
| Net chargeable transfer | 394,000 |
| Less nil band remaining £(325,000 – 60,000) | (265,000) |
|  | 129,000 |
| IHT @ 20/80 | 32,250 |

# BPP PRACTICE ASSESSMENT 2
# PERSONAL TAX

**Time allowed: 2.5 hours**

# Personal Tax (PLTX)
# BPP practice assessment 2

In the live assessment you will have access to the tax tables and reference material which have been reproduced at the back of this Question Bank. Please use them while completing this practice assessment so that you are familiar with their content.

## Task 1 (10 marks)

You work for a small firm of Chartered Accountants. A friend of yours has been looking for a property to rent for a while and has been telling you about this person they met a few days ago. It turns out that this person is one of your clients (you do not disclose this to your friend), and your friend tells you about the 20 different properties that this person has. You know that this client has one rental property and that is all that has been disclosed on their tax return.

**(a)** Using the AAT guidelines 'professional conduct in relation to taxation', explain what steps you should take regarding this information.

**(8 marks)**

**(b)** Which fundamental principle does the following describe? (Please use the picklist below part (c) to answer this question) **(1 mark)**

To maintain professional knowledge and skill at the level required to ensure that a client or employer receives competent professional service based on current developments in practice, legislation and techniques and acts diligently and in accordance with applicable technical and professional standards.

**(c)** Discussing client affairs with your friend in the pub who is thinking of investing in the client's company would be a breach of which fundamental principle? **(1 mark)**

**Picklist for questions (b) and (c)**

Confidentiality
Integrity
Objectivity
Professional behaviour
Professional competence and due care

## Task 2 (8 marks)

**(a)** Steel Ltd provides Susan with two company cars during 2020/21 for private and business use. The first car cost £13,800 when new (registered in 2018), has $CO_2$ emissions of 93g/km and has a diesel engine. The second car has a list price of £12,000 (registered in September 2020), has $CO_2$ emissions of 81g/km and has a diesel engine which meets the RDE2 standards. Susan used the first car for the first 7 months of 2020/21, and the second car for the remaining 5 months. Steel Ltd pays for all the running costs which amount to £950 for the first car and £735 for the second car. Steel also paid for private fuel for the second car, however Susan had to contribute £20 per month towards this.

**(5 marks)**

**(1)** **The scale charge percentage for the first car is:**

|  | % |
|---|---|

**(2)** **The taxable benefit for the first car is:**

| £ |  |
|---|---|

**(3)** **The scale charge percentage for the second car is:**

|  | % |
|---|---|

**(4)** **The taxable benefit for the second car is:**

| £ |  |
|---|---|

**(5)** **The fuel benefit for the second car is:**

| £ |  |
|---|---|

**(b)** Matthew is provided with a company van for the whole of 2020/21. The only private use of the van is the commute from home to work. **(3 marks)**

The taxable benefit for use of the van is:

| £ |  |
|---|---|

James is provided with a zero emissions van for the whole of 2020/21. He does not own a vehicle personally and so he uses the van for both business and private purposes. James pays for all the private fuel.

The taxable benefit for use of the van is:

| £ |  |
|---|---|

Luke is provided with a company van on 6th April 2020 which he uses for both personal and business purposes. The company pays for all of the fuel. He was made redundant on 6th October 2020 and he returned the van to the company on that date.

The taxable benefit for use of the van and private fuel is:

£ 

## Task 3 (8 marks)

**(a)** **Which ONE of the following is not a wholly exempt employment benefit?** **(1 mark)**

| | ✓ |
|---|---|
| Long service award worth £900 to employee with 30 years of service | |
| Workplace parking | |
| Workplace childcare facilities | |
| Moving expenses of £10,000 | |

**(b)** **For each of the following benefits provided to Emily by her employer Bloom Ltd, calculate the amount of the taxable benefit for 2020/21. If a benefit is exempt, enter 0.** **(3 marks)**

**(1)** Bloom Ltd gave Emily a loan on 1 August 2020 of £6,000 to pay for home improvements. Emily pays the company 1% interest on the loan but has not repaid any of the loan itself.

**The taxable benefit for 2020/21 is:**

£ 

**(2)** On 1 May 2020 Bloom Ltd provided her with a mobile telephone costing £150 for private and business use.

**The taxable benefit for 2020/21 is:**

£

**(c)** Bella's employer provided her with a house on 1 April 2020, when it was valued at £125,000. The employer had bought the house for £80,000 on 1 April 2009. The annual value of the house is £1,500. Bella pays £75 a month to the employer for the use of the house. She is also provided with new furniture valued at £15,000 on 1 April 2020. **(4 marks)**

**(1)** The basic accommodation benefit for 2020/21 is:

£ 

**(2)** The cost of providing the accommodation for calculating the additional benefit is:

£ 

**(3)** The additional accommodation benefit for 2020/21 is:

£ 

**(4)** The benefit for provision of furniture for 2020/21 is:

£ 

## Task 4 (6 marks)

**(a)** Sarah is a higher rate taxpayer and receives total dividends of £7,500 during 2020/21. Complete the following sentences. **(3 marks)**

**(1)** The amount of the dividend not taxed at 0% is:

£ 

**(2)** The tax rate applicable to the amount in (1) is:

% 

**(3)** The income tax payable on the dividend income is (to the nearest £1):

£ 

**(b)** Paul is a basic rate taxpayer and receives interest of £5,000 from an ISA and £3,500 of building society interest during 2020/21.

Complete the following sentences. **(3 marks)**

**(1)** His personal savings allowance is:

£

**(2)** **His taxable savings income after the savings allowance is:**

£ [    ]

**(3)** **The income tax payable on his savings income for 2020/21 is:**

£ [    ]

........................................................................

## Task 5 (6 marks)

**(a)** Demi bought two properties on 1 July 2020.

Property 1 was let unfurnished from 1 September 2020 at an annual rent of £12,000 payable monthly in arrears. The rent due on 31 March 2021 was not received until 14 April 2021.

The following were expenses paid by Demi on the property:

|  |  | £ |
| --- | --- | --- |
| 1 July 2020 | Insurance for the year ended 30 June 2021 | 700 |
| 8 Sept 2020 | Accountancy fees | 100 |
| 25 January 2021 | Re-painting the exterior of the property | 400 |

Property 2 was let furnished from 1 August 2020 at an annual rent of £9,000 payable annually in advance.

The following were expenses paid by Demi on the property:

|  |  | £ |
| --- | --- | --- |
| 1 July 2020 | Insurance for the year ended 30 June 2021 | 800 |
| 31 March 2021 | Redecoration | 900 |
| 3 April 2021 | Purchase of replacement carpets and curtains | 600 |

Using the proforma layout provided, calculate Demi's property income for the tax year 2020/21 by filling in the unshaded boxes. Add zeros if necessary. Both brackets and minus signs can be used to show negative numbers. **(4 marks)**

|  | Property 1 £ | Property 2 £ |
|---|---|---|
| Rental income |  |  |
| Property 1 |  |  |
| Property 2 |  |  |
| Less expenses |  |  |
| Insurance |  |  |
| Accountancy |  |  |
| Repainting |  |  |
| Redecoration |  |  |
| Replacement carpets and curtains |  |  |
| Net income |  |  |
| Total property income 2020/21 |  |  |

**(b)    On which expenditure could Demi claim replacement furniture relief? (Tick all that apply)                    (2 marks)**

|  | ✓ |
|---|---|
| A new fridge to replace the one that stopped working last week |  |
| A television for the new conservatory |  |
| New carpet for the living room after the old one was damaged in the recent floods |  |
| New crockery for the kitchen to replace the chipped plates and bowls |  |

## Task 6 (12 marks)

**(a)** Donald has the following amounts of taxable income for 2020/21:

Non-savings income £152,395 (PAYE deducted £52,000)
Savings income £145
Dividend income £210

**Donald's tax liability on each source of income for 2020/21 is as follows:** **(6 marks)**

**(1)   Non-savings income:**

£ 

**(2)   Savings income:**

£ 

**(3)   Dividend income:**

£ 

**(4)   Donald's tax payable for 2020/21 is:**

£ 

**(b)** You have received the following email from Serena Miles:

| | |
|---|---|
| **From:** | SMiles@webmail.net |
| **To:** | AATStudent@boxmail.net |
| **Sent:** | 30 November 2021 |
| **Subject:** | Pensions |

I currently don't have a pension and I am worried about this. I have two options. My employer, ABC plc, has said that I can join their occupational pension scheme. This would involve me paying 5% of my basic salary, and they would pay another 7%. However, I don't know how long I am going to continue to work for them.

Alternatively, I am thinking of taking out a private pension, possibly paying about 6% of my earnings into it.

However, I have no idea about the tax implications of these schemes. Would I get tax relief, and if so, how?

I hope you can help.

Serena

**WITHOUT discussing the merits of each scheme, advise Serena on the tax implications of an occupational pension scheme and a private pension scheme.** **(6 marks)**

| From: | AATStudent@boxmail.net |
| To: | SMiles@webmail.net |
| Sent: | 1 December 2021 |
| Subject: | Pensions |

# Task 7 (4 marks)

**(a)** (2 marks)

Your client Jackie received the following income in 2020/21:

|  | £ |
|---|---|
| Trading income | 20,000 |
| Property income | 5,000 |
| Building society interest | 145 |
| Interest from government stocks | 180 |
| Dividends from an ISA | 204 |
| Dividends | 210 |

**(1) Jackie's total non-savings income for 2020/21 is:**

£ [            ]

**(2) Jackie's total savings income for 2020/21 is:**

£ [            ]

**(2) Jackie's total dividend income for 2020/21 is:**

£ [            ]

**(b)** Sandy works for Geese Ltd. She is paid monthly and has an annual salary of £48,000. In March 2021 she received a bonus of £10,000.

(2 marks)

**Sandy's Class 1 employee's national insurance contributions for 2020/21 were (tick ONE):**

|  | ✓ |
|---|---|
| £5,020 |  |
| £6,791 |  |
| £4,837 |  |
| £5,820 |  |

## Task 8 (7 marks)

Mr and Mrs Shah are thinking of buying a property to rent out. Mrs Shah is a stay at home mum with no income and Mr Shah is a higher rate taxpayer. Mrs Shah has savings in an ISA that she accumulated whilst she was working full time.

**Suggest ways in which Mr and Mrs Shah could arrange this purchase in order to save tax for them as a couple.**

This style of task would be human marked in the exam.

## Task 9 (10 marks)

(a) **Classify whether a disposal of each of the following assets will be chargeable to or exempt from capital gains tax:   (4 marks)**

| Asset | Chargeable | Exempt |
|---|---|---|
| Shares in XYZ plc held in an ISA | | |
| Ruby necklace valued at £100,000 | | |
| Vintage Rolls Royce Car | | |
| Factory used in a trade | | |

**(b)** Trevor bought a 5-acre plot of land for £50,000. He sold 3 acres of the land at auction for £105,000 in August 2020. He had spent £2,500 installing drainage on the 3 acres which he sold. His disposal costs were £1,500. The market value of the remaining 2 acres at the date of sale was £45,000.

**The gain on sale of the 3 acres is:**                **(4 marks)**

| | ✓ |
|---|---|
| £66,000 | |
| £66,750 | |
| £67,500 | |
| £70,000 | |

**(c)**                                          **(2 marks)**

**(1)** Matt bought a picture for £7,000 and had costs of acquisition of £300. He sold it in August 2020 for £4,500 and had costs of disposal of £200.

**The allowable loss on sale is: (either show the loss by using brackets or a minus sign)**

| £ | |
|---|---|

**(2)** Keith bought a greyhound for £5,000. It won a number of races and he sold it for £7,000 in December 2020, incurring costs of disposal of £250.

**The chargeable gain on sale is:**

| | ✓ |
|---|---|
| Nil | |
| £1,667 | |
| £1,250 | |
| £1,750 | |

## Task 10 (10 marks)

Lee had the following transactions in shares in Snowy Ltd:

| Acquisitions | No of shares | Cost £ |
| --- | --- | --- |
| December 2006 | 10,000 | 10,800 |
| August 2007 | Bonus, 1 for 1 | Nil |
| June 2011 | 10,000 | 8,700 |
| December 2011 | Rights Issue, 1 for 10 | 40p each |

| Disposal | | Proceeds £ |
| --- | --- | --- |
| September 2020 | 15,000 | 18,650 |

**Using the proforma layout provided, calculate the chargeable gain made on the disposal of the shares in Snowy Ltd, and show the balance of shares to be carried forward for future disposal. Fill in all unshaded boxes, enter 0 if appropriate. Both brackets and minus signs can be used to show negative numbers.**

**Gain**

| | £ |
| --- | --- |
| Proceeds of sale | 18,650 |
| Less cost | 9,409 |
| Chargeable gain | 9241 |

**Share pool**

| | No of shares | Cost £ |
|---|---|---|
| December 2006 Acquisition | 10,000 | 10,800 |
| August 2007 Bonus issue | 10,000 | – |
| | 20,000 | 10,860 |
| June 2011 Acquisition | 10,000 | 8,700 |
| | 30,000 | 19,500 |
| December 2011 Rights issue | 3,000 | 1,200 |
| | 33,000 | 20,700 |
| September 2020 Disposal | 15,000 | (9,409) |
| c/f | 18,000 | 11,291 |

## Task 11 (7 marks)

Irma had the following chargeable gains in 2020/21:

| Gain on sale of shares August 2020 | £9,341 |
|---|---|
| Gain on sale of furniture February 2021 | £4,167 |
| She had allowable losses brought forward of | £1,000 |

Irma is an additional rate taxpayer.

**(a)** **Irma's taxable gains for 2020/21 are:**

£ 208

**(b)** **Irma's CGT payable for 2020/21 is:**

£ 42

**(c)** **Irma's CGT is due for payment by: (enter date as xx/xx/xxxx)**

£ 31/61/22

## Task 12 (6 marks)

**(a)** Gillian owned a 70% shareholding in R Ltd, an unquoted investment company. On 23 July 2020, she gave a 20% shareholding in R Ltd to her son. The values of shareholdings in R Ltd on 23 July 2020 were as follows:

|  | £ |
| --- | --- |
| 100% shareholding | 600,000 |
| 70% shareholding | 350,000 |
| 50% shareholding | 200,000 |
| 20% shareholding | 80,000 |

**What is the diminution in value of Gillian's estate as a result of her gift on 23 July 2020?** **(3 marks)**

|  | ✓ |
| --- | --- |
| £150,000 |  |
| £270,000 |  |
| £80,000 |  |
| £120,000 |  |

**(b)** Joel and Sunita were a married couple. Sunita died in July 2008 and 65% of her nil rate band of £312,000 (2008/09) was unused. Joel died in May 2020. He had made a potentially exempt transfer (after all available exemptions) of £75,000 in August 2016. Joel left his estate to his sister. Any relevant elections were made.

**What is the nil rate band available to set against Joel's death estate?** **(3 marks)**

|  | ✓ |
| --- | --- |
| £325,000 |  |
| £452,800 |  |
| £461,250 |  |
| £536,250 |  |

## Task 13 (6 marks)

**(a)** Mary made the following gifts in the tax year 2020/21:

(1)   £1,000 on the first day of each month for nine months to her niece to pay university living expenses. Mary used income surplus to her living requirements to make these payments.

(2)   £200 to her grandson on his birthday and a further £250 to the same grandson as a Christmas gift.

**Ignoring the annual exemption, what is the total value of potentially exempt transfers made by Mary as a result of these gifts?** **(1 mark)**

|  | ✓ |
|---|---|
| £9,450 |  |
| £200 |  |
| £9,000 |  |
| £450 |  |

**(b)** Georgia owns the following assets:

(1)   Her home valued at £774,000 with an outstanding mortgage of £160,000.

(2)   Vintage motor cars valued at £172,000.

(3)   Investments in Individual Savings Accounts valued at £97,000.

Georgia owes £22,400 in respect of a personal loan from a bank, and she has also verbally promised to pay legal fees of £4,600 incurred by her nephew. Her reasonable funeral expenses will amount to £5,500.

Georgia's husband died on 12 March 2009, and 70% of his inheritance tax nil rate band was not used.

Georgia has only made one lifetime gift of £100,000 in March 2017 to her son, and in her will she left her entire estate to her son.

**Calculate the inheritance tax due as a result of Georgia's death in 2020/21.** **(5 marks)**

This style of task would be human marked in the exam.

# BPP PRACTICE ASSESSMENT 2
# PERSONAL TAX

## ANSWERS

# Personal Tax (PLTX)
## BPP practice assessment 2

## Task 1 (10 marks)

**(a)** Firstly, it needs to be established whether this information is correct. Then, if this information is correct, the client needs to be approached.

If the client confirms this information to be correct and agrees to disclose this income to HMRC then the client needs to be advised of any penalties, interest, surcharges and other consequences.

If the client refuses to disclose this income to HMRC then you must cease to act for the client and inform HMRC that you no longer act for the client. However, because of the fundamental principle of confidentiality you would not need to disclose the reason for ceasing to act to HMRC.

This may be a money laundering issue and so this should be reported to your Money Laundering Officer. **(8 marks)**

**(b)** | Professional competence and due care ▼ |

**(c)** | Confidentiality ▼ |

## Task 2 (8 marks)

**(a)** **(5 marks)**

**(1)** The scale charge percentage for the first car is:

| 27 | % |

14% + (90 – 55)/5% + 4% + 2%

**(2)** The taxable benefit for the first car is:

| £ | 2,174 |

£13,800 × 27% × 7/12

**(3)** The scale charge percentage for the second car is:

| 19 | % |

14% + (80 – 55)/5%

**(4)**   The taxable benefit for the second car is:

| £ | 950 |
|---|-----|

£12,000 × 19% × 5/12

**(5)**   The fuel benefit for the second car is:

| £ | 1,940 |
|---|-------|

£24,500 × 19% × 5/12

There is no deduction for contribution towards private fuel.

**(b)**                                                                      **(3 marks)**

The taxable benefit for use of the van is:

| £ | Nil |
|---|-----|

The taxable benefit for use of the van and private fuel is:

| £ | 2,792 |
|---|-------|

(£3,490 × 80%)

The taxable benefit for use of the van and private fuel is:

| £ | 2,078 |
|---|-------|

(£3,490 + £666) × 6/12

# Task 3 (8 marks)

**(a)**

|  | ✓ |
|---|---|
| Long service award worth £900 to employee with 30 years of service |  |
| Workplace parking |  |
| Workplace childcare facilities |  |
| Moving expenses of £10,000 | ✓ |

Moving expenses of £10,000 are only exempt up to £8,000, the excess is taxable.

The long service award is wholly exempt as it is within the limit of £50 for each year of service and the period of service is in excess of 20 years.

**(b)** **(1)** The taxable benefit for 2020/21 is:

£ | 0

No taxable benefit arises if the combined outstanding balance on all loans to the employee did not exceed £10,000 at any time in the tax year.

**(2)** The taxable benefit for 2020/21 is:

£ | 0

Exempt

**(c)** **(1)** The basic accommodation benefit for 2020/21 is:

£ | 600

|  | £ |
|---|---|
| Annual value | 1,500 |
| Less payment by employee £75 × 12 = | (900) |
| Basic accommodation benefit | 600 |

**(2)** The cost of providing the accommodation for calculating the additional benefit is:

£ | 125,000

Market value at provision (acquired more than 6 years before provision)

**(3)** The additional accommodation benefit for 2020/21 is:

£ | 1,125

Excess of £125,000 over £75,000 = £50,000 × 2.25%

**(4)** The benefit for provision of furniture for 2020/21 is:

£ | 3,000

£15,000 × 20%

## Task 4 (6 marks)

**(a)** **(1)** The amount of the dividend not taxed at 0% is:

| £ | 5,500 |
|---|-------|

£7,500 – £2,000

**(2)** The tax rate applicable to the amount in (1) is:

| 32.5 | % |
|------|---|

She is a higher rate taxpayer

**(3)** The income tax payable on the dividend income is (to the nearest £1)

| £ | 1,788 |
|---|-------|

£5,500 × 32.5%

**(b)** **(1)** His personal savings allowance is:

| £ | 1,000 |
|---|-------|

Paul is a basic rate taxpayer

**(2)** His taxable savings income after the savings allowance is:

| £ | 2,500 |
|---|-------|

ISA interest is exempt. BSI £3,500 – £1,000 = £2,500

**(3)** The income tax payable on his savings income for 2020/21 is:

| £ | 500 |
|---|-----|

£2,500 × 20% = £500

## Task 5 (6 marks)

**(a)**

|  | Property 1 £ | Property 2 £ |
| --- | --- | --- |
| Rental income |  |  |
| Property 1 £12,000/12 × 6 | 6,000 |  |
| Property 2 |  | 9,000 |
| Less expenses |  |  |
| Insurance | (700) | (800) |
| Accountancy | (100) | 0 |
| Repainting | (400) | 0 |
| Redecoration | 0 | (900) |
| Replacement carpets and curtains | 0 | (600) |
| Net income | 4,800 | 6,700 |
| Total property income 2020/21 | 11,500 | |

**(b)**

|  | ✓ |
| --- | --- |
| A new fridge to replace the one that stopped working last week | ✓ |
| A television for the new conservatory |  |
| New carpet for the living room after the old one was damaged in the recent floods | ✓ |
| New crockery for the kitchen to replace the chipped plates and bowls | ✓ |

The television is not a replacement as the conservatory is new and therefore there would not have been one there before.

## Task 6 (12 marks)

**(a)** **(1)** Non-savings income:

| £ | 53,578 |
|---|---|

| | £ |
|---|---|
| £37,500 × 20% | 7,500 |
| £112,500 × 40% | 45,000 |
| £2,395 × 45% | 1,078 |
| £152,395 | 53,578 |

**(2)** Savings income:

| £ | 65 |
|---|---|

£145 × 45% (Additional rate taxpayers do not get a personal savings allowance)

**(3)** Dividend income:

| £ | 0 |
|---|---|

This is covered by the dividend allowance.

**(4)** Donald's tax payable for 2020/21 is:

| £ | 1,643 |
|---|---|

| | £ |
|---|---|
| Income tax liability £(53,578 + 65 + 0) | 53,643 |
| PAYE | (52,000) |
| Income tax payable | 1,643 |

**(b)**

| | |
|---|---|
| **From:** | AATStudent@boxmail.net |
| **To:** | SMiles@webmail.net |
| **Sent:** | 1 December 2021 |
| **Subject:** | Pensions |

Occupational pension schemes operate by the employer deducting your pension contribution from your salary before the PAYE is calculated. In your case this would be 5%. This means that full tax relief is automatically obtained at source at your applicable rate of tax. The employer is responsible for paying over the pension payments to the pension provider.

The 7% that your employer pays to the pension scheme on your behalf has no tax implications for you, ie this will not be classed as a taxable benefit.

Private pension schemes work quite differently. You pay the pension provider direct, usually monthly. The amount you pay is net of basic rate tax.

So, if for example, you decide you would like to put £100 a month into your pension, you only actually have to pay in £80, HM Revenue & Customs will pay the other £20. This automatically provides you with 20% tax relief.

If you are a higher or additional rate taxpayer, you will be entitled to further tax relief. In order to get tax relief at the higher rate of 40% or the additional rate of 45%, the basic rate band (and also the additional rate threshold) is extended by the gross pension contributions so that the 40% and 45% tax rates will apply after the pension has been adjusted for.

## Task 7 (4 marks)

**(a)** **(1)** Jackie's total non-savings income for 2020/21 is:

| £ | 25,000 |
|---|---|

£20,000 + £5,000

**(2)** Jackie's total savings income for 2020/21 is:

| £ | 325 |
|---|---|

£145 + £180 = £325

**(3)** Jackie's total dividend income for 2020/21 is:

| £ | 210 |
|---|---|

Dividends from ISAs are exempt.

**(b)** Sandy's Class 1 Employee's national insurance contributions for 2020/21 were:

| | ✓ |
|---|---|
| £5,020 | |
| £6,791 | |
| £4,837 | ✓ |
| £5,820 | |

**Workings**

£(48,000/12) = £4,000 per month
£(4,000 – 792) = 3,208 × 12% × 11 months =       4,235
£(4,167 – 792) = 3,375 × 12% × 1 month =       405
£(14,000 – 4,167) = 9,833 × 2% × 1 month =       197
                                                    £4,837

The answer £5,020 calculates the NICs on an annual basis ie as if Sandy were a director. The answers £6,791 calculates employer's NIC The answer £5,820 taxes everything over the employee threshold at 12%.

# Task 8 (7 marks)

As Mrs Shah has savings but no income at present, she is not paying any tax. Any interest she receives from her ISA is exempt from Income Tax.

Mr Shah is a higher rate tax payer who would pay 40% income tax on any rents received.

The rental income would be allocated between them based on their percentage ownership.

Mr and Mrs Shah should arrange the purchase so that Mrs Shah receives as much rent as possible so that she uses her personal allowance. Any income above her personal allowance would be taxed at 20%.

This would mean that the first £12,500 of the income would not be taxable as it would be covered by her personal allowance and anything above that would be taxed at 20% in her hands as opposed to 40% if Mr Shah received it.

# Task 9 (10 marks)

**(a)**

| Asset | Chargeable | Exempt |
|---|---|---|
| Shares in XYZ plc held in an ISA | | ✓ |
| Ruby necklace valued at £100,000 | ✓ | |
| Vintage Rolls Royce Car | | ✓ |
| Factory used in a trade | ✓ | |

**(b)**

| | ✓ |
|---|---|
| £66,000 | ✓ |
| £66,750 | |
| £67,500 | |
| £70,000 | |

| | £ |
|---|---|
| Proceeds of sale | 105,000 |
| Less costs of disposal | (1,500) |
| Net proceeds | 103,500 |
| Less cost | |
| (105,000/105,000 + 45,000) × £50,000 | (35,000) |
| enhancement expenditure | (2,500) |
| Chargeable gain | 66,000 |

The answer £66,750 calculates the part disposal on cost plus enhancement expenditure. The answer £67,500 ignores costs of disposal. The answer £70,000 ignores costs and enhancement expenditure.

**(c) (1)** The allowable loss on sale is:

£ | (1,500)

| | £ |
|---|---|
| Deemed disposal proceeds | 6,000 |
| Less costs of disposal | (200) |
| Net deemed disposal proceeds | 5,800 |
| Less cost £(7,000 + 300) | (7,300) |
| Allowable loss | (1,500) |

**(2)**

| | ✓ |
|---|---|
| Nil | ✓ |
| £1,667 | |
| £1,250 | |
| £1,750 | |

The greyhound is a wasting chattel and so is an exempt asset. Therefore, there is no chargeable gain on the disposal.

---

## Task 10 (10 marks)

**Gain**

| | £ |
|---|---|
| Proceeds of sale | 18,650 |
| Less cost | (9,409) |
| Chargeable gain | 9,241 |

## Share pool

|  | No of shares | Cost £ |
|---|---|---|
| December 2006 Acquisition | 10,000 | 10,800 |
| August 2007 Bonus 1 for 1 | 10,000 | 0 |
|  | 20,000 | 10,800 |
| June 2011 Acquisition | 10,000 | 8,700 |
|  | 30,000 | 19,500 |
| December 2011 Rights 1 for 10 × £0.40 | 3,000 | 1,200 |
|  | 33,000 | 20,700 |
| September 2020 Disposal (15,000/33,000 × £20,700) | (15,000) | (9,409) |
| c/f | 18,000 | 11,291 |

..................................................................................

# Task 11 (7 marks)

**(a)** Irma's taxable gains for 2020/21 are:

| £ | 208 |
|---|---|

|  | £ |
|---|---|
| Gain on shares | 9,341 |
| Gain on furniture | 4,167 |
| Net chargeable gains | 13,508 |
| Less annual exempt amount | (12,300) |
| Less loss brought forward | (1,000) |
| Taxable gains | 208 |

**(b)** Irma's CGT payable for 2020/21 is:

| £ | 42 |
|---|---|

£208 × 20%

**(c)** Irma's CGT is due for payment by:

| 31/01/2022 |
|---|

........................................................................

## Task 12 (6 marks)

**(a)**

|  | ✓ |
|---|---|
| £150,000 | ✓ |
| £270,000 | |
| £80,000 | |
| £120,000 | |

**Workings**

|  | £ |
|---|---|
| Before the gift: 70% shareholding | 350,000 |
| After the gift: 50% shareholding | (200,000) |
| Transfer of value | 150,000 |

The answer £270,000 is the value of a 70% shareholding less the value of a 20% shareholding. The answer £80,000 is the value of a 20% shareholding. The answer £120,000 is 20% of the value of a 100% holding.

**(b)**

|  | ✓ |
|---|---|
| £325,000 | |
| £452,800 | |
| £461,250 | ✓ |
| £536,250 | |

**Workings**

|  | £ |
| --- | --- |
| Sunita's unused nil rate band £325,000 × 65% | 211,250 |
| Joel's nil rate band | 325,000 |
|  | 536,250 |
| Less used against Joel's PET now chargeable | (75,000) |
| Available nil rate band to set against Joel's death estate | 461,250 |

The answer £325,000 is the value of Joel's NRB only without adjustment. The answer £452,800 calculates Sunita's unused NRB based on the historic NRB amount. The answer £536,250 does not adjust for the PET.

## Task 13 (6 marks)

**(a)**

|  | ✓ |
| --- | --- |
| £9,450 |  |
| £200 |  |
| £9,000 |  |
| £450 | ✓ |

**Workings**

The gifts to the niece are exempt as normal expenditure out of income because they are part of the normal expenditure of the donor, made out of income and left the donor with sufficient income to maintain her usual standard of living.

The small gifts exemption only applies to gifts up to £250 per donee per tax year. If gifts total more than £250 the whole amount is chargeable. Since the gifts to the grandson totalled £(200 + 250) = £450 in 2020/21, this exemption does not apply.

**(b)** Inheritance tax due:

Death estate:

| | £ |
|---|---|
| Property | 774,000 |
| Less repayment mortgage | (160,000) |
| | 614,000 |
| Motor cars | 172,000 |
| Investments | 97,000 |
| Bank loan | (22,400) |
| Nephew's legal fees * | (0) |
| Funeral expenses | (5,500) |
| | 855,100 |
| Tax: | |
| Residence nil rate band: £175,000 + £175,000** × 0% | 0 |
| Nil band:  £458,500*** × 0% | 0 |
| £46,600 × 40% | 18,640 |
| Total IHT due | 18,640 |

* The promise to pay the nephew's legal fees is not deductible as it is purely gratuitous (not made for valuable consideration).

** Residence nil rate band of £175,000 (death in 2020/21) is available. Husband's deemed unused RNRB of £175,000 (as he died prior to 2017/18) can also be claimed.

*** Georgia's nil band: £(325,000 – (94,000 PET less 2xAEs)) 231,000

Unused nil band of husband: £(325,000 × 70%)           227,500

# BPP PRACTICE ASSESSMENT 3
# PERSONAL TAX

**Time allowed: 2.5 hours**

# Personal Tax (PLTX)
# BPP practice assessment 3

In the live assessment you will have access to the tax tables and reference material which have been reproduced at the back of this Question Bank. Please use them while completing this practice assessment so that you are familiar with their content.

## Task 1 (10 marks)

**(a)** You receive the following email from a client, who is a higher rate taxpayer.

| | |
|---|---|
| **From:** | Raman99@sherbet.net |
| **To:** | AATStudent@boxmail.net |
| **Sent:** | 20 June 2020 |
| **Subject:** | More information |

Hello, I am so sorry, I know that you have already sent in my tax form for 2019/20. Unfortunately, I forgot to tell you that I started letting out a property on 1 January 2020 and received £3,000 of rental income for the first three months.

I suggest we leave the 2019/20 return as it is, and I will just account for the income as if I started renting the property in April 2020.

Thanks.

Raman

**Reply to Raman's email.**

| | |
|---|---|
| **From:** | AATStudent@boxmail.net |
| **To:** | Raman99@sherbet.net |
| **Sent:** | 22 June 2020 |
| **Subject:** | More information |

**(b)** A client has told you that if you leave £50,000 of property income out of their tax return then they will let you spend a week in their holiday home in the Maldives.

Which two fundamental principles are under threat from this behaviour? (Please use the picklist below to answer this question)

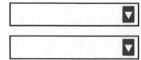

**Picklist:**

Confidentiality
Integrity
Objectivity
Professional behaviour
Professional competence and due care

## Task 2 (8 marks)

Khalid works for KML plc and is provided with a company car for business and private use from 6 June 2020.

The car has a diesel engine with $CO_2$ emissions of 117 g/km, which does not meet the RDE2 standards. The car was registered in May 2020. It has a list price of £27,000, although the company actually paid £23,500 for the car. Khalid agreed to make a capital contribution of £6,000 towards the cost of the car. The company pays for all running costs, including all fuel. Khalid pays £50 a month towards the cost of private fuel – the actual cost of private fuel is about £90 a month.

**(1)    The cost of the car in the taxable benefit computation is:**

|          | ✓ |
|----------|---|
| £21,000  |   |
| £22,000  |   |
| £17,500  |   |
| £18,500  |   |

**(2)    The percentage used in the taxable benefit computation is:**

|       | % |
|-------|---|

**(3)    The taxable benefit in respect of the provision of fuel for private use is:**

| £ |   |
|---|---|

**(4)    If a new diesel car costing £24,000 was provided to an employee on the 6 April 2020 (registered April 2020), has a CO2 rating of 84g/km and meets the RDE2 standards, the company car benefit for 2020/21 would be:**

| £ |   |
|---|---|

## Task 3 (8 marks)

**(a)** Lou is employed by Jane Quentin and receives the following benefits as a result of her employment.

**In each case enter the taxable benefit arising. Enter 0 if the benefit is not taxable.**

**(1)** An interest free loan of £10,500 made on 1 July 2020, no repayments made during 2020/21.

£ [          ]

**(2)** Cash voucher for £100 provided in December 2020. Jane acquired the voucher for £90.

£ [          ]

**(3)** Van for business and private use from 1 October 2020 onwards.

£ [          ]

**(4)** Fuel for van for private use from 1 January 2021 onwards.

£ [          ]

**(b)** **For each of the following benefits, tick whether they would be partly exempt or wholly exempt if received by an employee who is a basic rate taxpayer in 2020/21:**

| Benefit | Partly exempt | Wholly exempt |
|---|---|---|
| Staff party costing £125 per head | | |
| Mobile phone | | |
| Removal expenses of £10,000 | | |
| Work related training costing £1,500 | | |

**(c)** Madge is employed by V plc. She uses her own car for business purposes and is reimbursed 45p per mile by her employer. Madge travelled 15,000 miles on business in 2020/21.

**What are the employment income consequences of the reimbursement for business mileage?**

| | ✓ |
|---|---|
| £6,750 taxable benefit | |
| £1,000 taxable benefit | |
| No taxable benefit or allowable deduction | |
| £1,000 allowable deduction | |

## Task 4 (6 marks)

**(a)** A higher rate taxpayer receives £3,250 of bank interest, £250 of which was from his cash ISA, and £10,000 of dividends during 2020/21. What amounts will be liable to income tax at a rate of above 0% in 2020/21?

| | ✓ |
|---|---|
| £3,000 of interest and £8,000 of dividends | |
| £3,000 of interest and £10,000 of dividends | |
| £2,250 of interest and £8,000 of dividends | |
| £2,500 of interest and £8,000 of dividends | |

**(b)** Tick the relevant box to show which of the following types of income are chargeable to income tax and which are exempt from income tax:

| Source of income | Chargeable | Exempt |
|---|---|---|
| Individual Savings Account interest | | |
| Government stock interest | | |
| Dividends received from an Individual Savings Account | | |
| Bank deposit account interest | | |

# Task 5 (6 marks)

**(a)** Michaela rents out a house from 1 July 2020.

She charges a rent of £600 per month payable in arrears on the last day of each month. The tenants don't pay the rent due on 31 March 2021 until 10 April 2021.

Michaela also pays an insurance premium of £400 on 6 July 2020, covering the period 6 July 2020 to 5 July 2021.

Michaela has chosen to use the accruals basis to compute her property profits.

**(1)   The rental income taxable for 2020/21 is:**

£ [          ]

**(2)   The insurance premium allowable as an expense for 2020/21 is:**

£ [          ]

**(b)** Wilma owns two flats that she rents out. Flat A is unfurnished. Flat B is furnished. She has chosen to use the accruals basis to calculate her property profits.

The income and expenses for these properties are:

|                      | Flat A £ | Flat B £ |
|----------------------|----------|----------|
| **Monthly income:**  |          |          |
| Rent                 | 500      | 650      |
| **Annual expenses:** |          |          |
| Council tax          | 1,000    | 800      |
| Water rates          | 300      | 300      |
| Insurance            | 350      | 250      |

Flat A was fully occupied during 2020/21. However, the tenants in Flat B moved out in November 2020 having paid the rent to the end of that month. Wilma was unable to re-let the flat until June 2021.

Wilma spent £410 replacing various items of furniture for Flat B that had been damaged by the outgoing tenants.

Wilma had a loss of £1,200 on her income from property in 2019/20.

Using the proforma layout below, calculate Wilma's property income for 2020/21. Fill in all unshaded boxes, enter 0 if appropriate. Both brackets and minus signs can be used to show negative numbers.

| | Flat A £ | Flat B £ |
|---|---|---|
| Income | 6000 | 5200 |
| Expenses: | | |
| Council tax | (1000) | (800) |
| Water rates | (300) | (300) |
| Insurance | (350) | (250) |
| Replacement furniture relief | | 410 |
| Net income from property | 4350 | 3550 |
| Total property income | 7250 | |
| Less loss b/f | (1200) | |
| Taxable property income | 6550 | |

## Task 6 (12 marks)

(a) Guy has the following income for 2020/21:

| | £ |
|---|---|
| Employment income (PAYE £250) | 13,150 |
| Interest received from building societies | 46,250 |
| Dividends received | 14,000 |

**Calculate Guy's income tax payable for 2020/21 entering your answer and workings into the blank table below. Brackets or a minus sign are both acceptable when entering negative numbers.**

| | | | |
|---|---|---|---|
| Employment Income | 13,150 | | |
| Building Society Int | | 46,250 | |
| Dividends | | | 15,000 |
| Net Income | 13,150 | 46,250 | 14,001 |
| Personal Allowance | (12,500) | | |
| Taxable Income | 650 | 46,250 | 15,000 |
| 650 × 20% | 130 | | |
| (500 × 0%)+ | 0 | | |
| 36400 × 20% | 7280 | | |
| 9350 × 40% | 3740 | | |
| 2000 × 0% | 0 | | |
| 12,000 × 32.5% | 3900 | | |
| Tax Liability | 15,050 | | |
| Deducted at Source | (250) | | |
| | 14,800 | | |
| | | | |

**(b)** Guy is considering asking his employer to set up a small charitable donation of about £50 a month and deduct it out of his salary but is unsure if he will get any tax relief for this.

**Explain to Guy how he will get tax relief on such donations.**

204

## Task 7 (4 marks)

**What category of national insurance would be payable on a company car benefit, who is liable for this National Insurance and how much is the national insurance contribution on a benefit of £5,850?**

**(1)** Category of National Insurance

[                    ▼]

**(2)** Who is liable for this National Insurance?

[                    ▼]

**(3)** How much is the national insurance contribution? State your answer to the nearest £1.

£ [                    ]

**Picklist** for questions (b) (1) and (2)

Class 1 Employee
Class 1 Employer
Class 1 A
Employee
Employer

## Task 8 (7 marks)

**(a)** Owen is employed by X Ltd throughout 2020/21. He earns £55,000 a year. He also receives interest income from a Santander Bank current account.

**Owen could do the following to save tax:**

|  | True | False |
|---|---|---|
| Invest his savings in an ISA |  |  |
| Donate to charity under the Gift Aid scheme |  |  |
| Invest in a property |  |  |
| Contribute to a pension |  |  |
| Invest in a tax avoidance scheme set up by his friend |  |  |

**(b)** The following amounts were received in relation to Owen's employment:

   (1)   Monthly salary paid on the last working day of each month

   (2)   Tips of £300 paid by customers directly to Owen

   (3)   Employer's contribution of 6% of salary to company's occupational pension scheme

   (4)   Reimbursement of business expenses of £500

**For each item, tick the relevant column to indicate whether the item is taxable or not taxable:**

| Item | Taxable | Not taxable |
|---|---|---|
| Salary | | |
| Tips | | |
| Employer's pension contribution | | |
| Reimbursement of business expenses | | |

## Task 9 (10 marks)

**(a)   For each statement, tick the appropriate box in respect of the capital gains calculation.                                    (4 marks)**

| Disposal | Market value used | Actual proceeds used | No gain/no loss disposal |
|---|---|---|---|
| Olivia sells shares for £5,000 to her wife Lucy when they are worth £4,000 | √ | | |
| William sells land to his brother for £10,000 when it is worth £50,000 | √ | | |
| Zeta gives an asset worth £4,000 to her friend Tanya | | √ | |
| Olwyn sells listed shares for proceeds of £12,000 | | | |

**(b)** Melly bought a holiday cottage for £32,000, incurring legal costs of £600 on the purchase. She spent £6,000 on adding a conservatory to the cottage. This was destroyed during a storm in 2013 and not replaced. Melly sold the cottage in March 2021 for £45,000. She paid estate agent's fees of £900 and legal costs of £350.

The chargeable gain on sale is:

| £ | |
|---|---|

**(c)** **(1)** Suki purchased a vase for £9,500. In December 2020 she sold the vase at auction for £2,500. This amount is before deducting the auctioneer's 10% commission.

### The allowable loss on sale is:

| | ✓ |
|---|---|
| £3,750 | |
| £3,500 | |
| £7,000 | |
| £7,250 | |

**(2)** **A chattel with a useful life of 60 years or less is a wasting chattel.**

| | ✓ |
|---|---|
| True | |
| False | |

## Task 10 (10 marks)

Vernon sold 4,000 shares in R Ltd for £36,200 on 23 February 2021. He had acquired his holdings in R Ltd as follows:

| Date | Transaction | No of shares | £ |
|---|---|---|---|
| 14 April 2001 | Purchase | 6,000 | 18,400 |
| 29 May 2006 | Rights issue | 1 for 20 | £4 each |
| 10 March 2021 | Purchase | 500 | 3,400 |

**Using the proforma layout provided, compute the total gain on sale. Both brackets and minus signs can be used to show negative numbers.**

**Share pool**

| | No of shares | Cost £ |
|---|---|---|
| Apr 1001 Pur | 6000 | 18,400 |
| May 2006 Right 1/20 d/a | 300 | 1200 |
| | 6,300 | 19600 |
| Dispose (3,500)(6300×6.0 | (3,500) | (10,889) |
| | | |
| c/f | 2800 | 8711 |

**Total gain on sale**

| | £ |
|---|---|
| First match equition in the next | |
| Proceeds of sale $\frac{600}{4000} \times 31,200$ | 4525 |
| less allowble cost | (3,400) |
| Gain | 1,125 |
| Next match with shares in the sharepool | |
| Proceeds of sale $\frac{3500}{4,900} \times 51,200$ | 31,125 |
| Less allowable cost | (10,889) |
| Gain | 20,786 |
| Total Gains ( 1,125 + 20,786 | 21,911 |
| | |

## Task 11 (7 marks)

**(a)** Desmond bought a house in Glasgow on 1 April 2005. He lived in the house until 30 September 2008. He was then sent to work in Bristol by his employer, before returning to live in the house again on 1 October 2013. He lived in the house before moving out on 30 April 2014 to live with friends until the house was sold on 30 September 2020.

**Using the proforma layout provided, show which periods of ownership are exempt and which are chargeable matching the correct explanation for each period. (5 marks)**

| Explanation | | Exempt (dates) | | Chargeable (dates) | |
|---|---|---|---|---|---|
| Actual Occupation ▼ | | 1 Apr to Sep ▼ | | ▼ | |
| ▼ | | ▼ | | ▼ | |
| ▼ | | ▼ | | ▼ | |
| ▼ | | ▼ | | ▼ | |
| ▼ | | ▼ | | ▼ | |
| ▼ | | ▼ | | ▼ | |

| Picklist for explanation: | Picklist for dates: |
|---|---|
| Not occupied and not followed by actual occupation | 1 October 2008 to 30 September 2012 |
| Actual occupation | 1 May 2014 to 31 December 2019 |
| Actual occupation | 1 April 2005 to 30 September 2008 |
| Last nine months ownership | 1 October 2012 to 30 September 2013 |
| Up to three years any reason | 1 January 2020 to 30 September 2020 |
| Four years employed elsewhere in UK | 1 October 2013 to 30 April 2014 |

**(b)** Erin purchased a property for £210,000 on 1 April 2005 and received disposal proceeds of £385,000 on 30 September 2020. It is her main residence but she moved out on 1 July 2020.

**After applying private residence relief, the sale of Erin's house will result in a chargeable gain.**

| | ✓ |
|---|---|
| True | |
| False | |

**(c)** **Ciara sells an antique necklace in August 2020 which gives rise to capital gains tax payable of £3,500. By what date must Ciara pay this? (xx/xx/xxxx)**

| |
|---|

........................................................................................

## Task 12 (6 marks)

**(a)** Rodney died on 13 August 2020 leaving an estate worth £520,000. In his will he left £200 in cash to each of his five nephews, investments held in ISAs valued at £350,000 to his daughter, and the residue of his estate to his wife.

**What is the chargeable estate for inheritance tax purposes?**

| £ | |
|---|---|

**(b)** Kirstin gave shares to a trust on 15 September 2012 resulting in a gross chargeable transfer of £150,000 and shares worth £600,000 to her brother on 10 July 2017. Kirstin died on 23 October 2020.

**Ignoring the annual exemption, what is the inheritance tax payable on Kirstin's death in relation to her lifetime transfers?** (Assume the nil band has always been £325,000)

| | ✓ |
|---|---|
| £170,000 | |
| £88,000 | |
| £136,000 | |
| £110,000 | |

........................................................................................

## Task 13 (6 marks)

Jimmy died on 14 February 2021. He had used up his nil rate band at the date of his death by making the following gifts during his lifetime:

(1) On 2 August 2019 Jimmy made a cash gift to his grandson as a wedding gift when he got married.

(2) On 9 September 2019 Jimmy gave 200 shares valued at £5 each in J Ltd, an unquoted investment company, to his daughter. Before the gift, Jimmy owned 5,100 shares valued at £30 each in J Ltd. After the gift Jimmy owned 4,900 shares valued at £20 each in J Ltd.

(3) On 14 November 2019 Jimmy made a cash gift of £800,000 to a trust. Jimmy paid the inheritance tax arising from this gift.

**(a)** **What was the total amount of the exemptions that were deducted in computing the potentially exempt transfer made on 2 August 2019?**

| | ✓ |
|---|---|
| £3,000 | |
| £8,500 | |
| £6,000 | |
| £11,000 | |

**(b)** **What is the diminution in value in Jimmy's estate as a result of his gift on 9 September 2019?**

| | ✓ |
|---|---|
| £55,000 | |
| £4,000 | |
| £6,000 | |
| £1,000 | |

**(c)** **What was the amount of the lifetime inheritance tax paid by Jimmy as a result of his gift made on 14 November 2019?**

£ [          ]

# BPP PRACTICE ASSESSMENT 3
# PERSONAL TAX

## ANSWERS

## Personal Tax (PLTX)
## BPP practice assessment 3

### Task 1 (10 marks)

**(a)**

| | |
|---|---|
| **From:** | AATStudent@boxmail.net |
| **To:** | Raman99@sherbet.net |
| **Sent:** | 22 June 2021 |
| **Subject:** | More information |

Thank you for your email. Unfortunately, I cannot condone the action you have suggested as it amounts to tax evasion. By not declaring the income you are deliberately misleading HMRC resulting in an underpayment of your tax in 2019/20. Should they choose to look into your tax return and discover this omission you would be liable to interest and penalties.

Ultimately it is your choice and I can only advise you as to the correct course of action. However, if you choose not to take my advice then I would have to cease acting for you with regard to your tax affairs and inform HMRC that I have done so. I will not tell them why as this would be a breach of client confidentiality.

I hope it doesn't come to this. Please feel free to contact me to discuss this matter further.

**(b)**

| Integrity | ▼ |
|---|---|

| Professional behaviour | ▼ |
|---|---|

### Task 2 (8 marks)

**(1)** The cost of the car in the taxable benefit computation is:

| | ✓ |
|---|---|
| £21,000 | |
| £22,000 | ✓ |
| £17,500 | |
| £18,500 | |

List price £27,000 less capital contribution paid by employee (max) £5,000

The answer £21,000 deducts the total capital contribution paid. The answer £17,500 uses the amount actually paid less the total contribution. The answer £18,500 uses the amount actually paid less the restricted contribution.

**(2)** The percentage used in the taxable benefit computation is:

| 30 | % |
|---|---|

14% + (115 – 55)/5% + 4% (diesel) = 30%

**(3)** The taxable benefit in respect of the provision of fuel for private use is:

| £ | 6,125 |
|---|---|

£24,500 × 30% × 10/12 (There is no reduction for part reimbursement of private fuel).

**(4)** If a new diesel car costing £24,000 was provided to an employee on the 6 April 2020 (registered April 2020), has a $CO_2$ rating of 84g/km and meets the RDE2 standards, the company car benefit for 2020/21 would be:

| £ | 4,560 |
|---|---|

14% + (80 – 55)/5% = 19%
19% × £24,000

..........................................................................................

# Task 3 (8 marks)

**(a)** **(1)**

| £ | 177 |
|---|---|

£10,500 × 2.25% × 9/12

**(2)**

| £ | 100 |
|---|---|

**(3)**

| £ | 1,745 |
|---|---|

£3,490 × 6/12

**(4)**

| £ | 167 |
|---|---|

£666 × 3/12

**(b)**

| Benefit | Partly exempt | Wholly exempt |
|---|---|---|
| Staff party costing £125 per head | | ✓ |
| Mobile phone | | ✓ |
| Removal expenses of £10,000 | ✓<br>(up to £8,000) | |
| Work related training costing £1,500 | | ✓ |

**(c)**

| | ✓ |
|---|---|
| £6,750 taxable benefit | |
| £1,000 taxable benefit | ✓ |
| No taxable benefit or allowable deduction | |
| £1,000 allowable deduction | |

| | £ |
|---|---|
| Amount reimbursed 15,000 × 45p | 6,750 |
| Less statutory allowance | |
| 10,000 miles × 45p | (4,500) |
| 5,000 miles × 25p | (1,250) |
| Taxable benefit | 1,000 |

## Task 4 (6 marks)

**(a)**

| | ✓ |
|---|---|
| £3,000 of interest and £8,000 of dividends | |
| £3,000 of interest and £10,000 of dividends | |
| £2,250 of interest and £8,000 of dividends | |
| £2,500 of interest and £8,000 of dividends | ✓ |

The taxable interest is after deduction of the savings allowance (£500 for higher rate tax payers) and excludes the ISA interest. £3,250 – £250 – £500 = £2,500. The first £2,000 of dividends are taxable at 0% for all taxpayers.

**(b)**

| Source of income | Chargeable | Exempt |
|---|---|---|
| Individual Savings Account interest | | ✓ |
| Government stock interest | ✓ | |
| Dividends received from an Individual Savings Account | | ✓ |
| Bank deposit account interest | ✓ | |

. . . . . . . . . . . . . . . . . . . . . . . . . . . . . . . . . . . . . . . . . . . . . . . . . . . . . . . . . . . . . . . . . . . . . . . . . . . . . . . . . . .

## Task 5 (6 marks)

**(a)** **(1)** The rental income taxable for 2020/21 is:

| £ | 5,400 |
|---|---|

Rental income accrued 2020/21:

1 July 2020 to 31 March 2021 (working in whole months)

9 months × £600 per month

The actual date of receipt of the rent due on 31 March 2021 is not relevant when using the accruals basis.

**(2)** The insurance premium allowable as an expense for 2020/21 is:

| £ | 300 |
|---|---|

£400 × 9/12

**(b)**

| | Flat A £ | Flat B £ |
|---|---|---|
| Income: £500 × 12/ £650 × 8 | 6,000 | 5,200 |
| Expenses: | | |
| Council tax | (1,000) | (800) |
| Water rates | (300) | (300) |
| Insurance | (350) | (250) |
| Replacement furniture relief | (0) | (410) |
| Net income from property | 4,350 | 3,440 |
| Total property income £(4,350 + 3,440) | 7,790 | |
| Less loss b/f | (1,200) | |
| Taxable property income | 6,590 | |

## Task 6 (12 marks)

**(a)**

| | Non savings income £ | Savings income £ | Dividend income £ |
|---|---|---|---|
| Employment income | 13,150 | | |
| Building society interest | | 46,250 | |
| Dividends | | | 14,000 |
| Personal allowance | (12,500) | | |
| Taxable income | 650 | 46,250 | 14,000 |
| **Income tax** | | | |
| £650 × 20% | | | 130 |
| £500 × 0% (savings allowance) | | | 0 |
| £36,350 (£37,500 – £650 – £500) × 20% | | | 7,270 |
| £9,400 (£46,250 – £500 – 36,350) × 40% | | | 3,760 |
| £2,000 × 0% | | | 0 |
| £12,000 × 32.5% | | | 3,900 |
| Income tax liability | | | 15,060 |
| Less tax deducted at source: | | | |
| PAYE | | | (250) |
| Income tax payable | | | 14,810 |

**(b)**

Guy's employer will deduct the donation from his salary before it is taxed. If he decides to pay £50 a month, this will mean he will get tax relief during the year on £600 (£50 × 12). This will reduce his taxable employment income to £50.

**Note.** You would not be expected to recalculate the tax here but for information the calculation would be as follows:

| Income tax | |
|---|---:|
| £50 × 20% | 10 |
| £500 × 0% | 0 |
| £36,950 (£37,500 – 50 – 500) × 20% | 7,390 |
| £8,800 (£46,250 – £36,950 – £500) × 40% | 3,520 |
| £2,000 × 0% + £12,000 × 32.5% (as above) | 3,900 |
| Income tax liability | 14,820 |

Tax saving £15,060 – £14,820 = £240

This seems a large saving on a £600 reduction in income (40%!) but can be explained:

£600 employment income which would have been taxed at 20% is not taxed at all, saving £120.

£600 of savings income is now taxed at 20% rather than 40% saving another £120.

## Task 7 (4 marks)

**(1)** Category of national insurance

| Class 1A |
|---|

**(2)** Who is liable for this national insurance?

| Employer |
|---|

**(3)** How much is the national insurance contribution? State your answer to the nearest £1.

| £ | 807 |
|---|---|

£5,850 × 13.8%

........................................................................................

## Task 8 (7 marks)

**(a)**

|  | True | False |
|---|---|---|
| Invest his savings in an ISA | ✓ |  |
| Donate to charity under the Gift Aid scheme | ✓ |  |
| Invest in a property |  | ✓ |
| Contribute to a pension | ✓ |  |
| Invest in a tax avoidance scheme set up by his friend |  | ✓** |

*Investing in a property would not save tax as the rental income would be taxable as non-savings income.

**Investing in a tax avoidance scheme is risky and whilst it may save tax initially it could end up not saving tax if HMRC decide to close down the scheme.

**(b)**

| Item | Taxable | Not taxable |
|---|---|---|
| Salary | ✓ |  |
| Tips | ✓ |  |
| Employer's pension contribution |  | ✓ |
| Reimbursement of business expenses |  | ✓ |

........................................................................................

# Task 9 (10 marks)

**(a)**

| Disposal | Market value used | Actual proceeds used | No gain/no loss disposal |
|---|:---:|:---:|:---:|
| Olivia sells shares for £5,000 to her wife Lucy when they are worth £4,000 | | | ✓ |
| William sells land to his brother for £10,000 when it is worth £50,000 | ✓ | | |
| Zeta gives an asset worth £4,000 to her friend Tanya | ✓ | | |
| Olwyn sells listed shares for proceeds of £12,000 | | ✓ | |

**(b)**  The chargeable gain on sale is:

£ | 11,150

| | £ |
|---|---:|
| Proceeds of sale | 45,000 |
| Less disposal costs £(900 + 350) | (1,250) |
| Net proceeds of sale | 43,750 |
| Less costs of acquisition £(32,000 + 600) | (32,600) |
| enhancement expenditure(not reflected in value of property on disposal) | (Nil) |
| Chargeable gain | 11,150 |

**(c)** **(1)** The allowable loss on sale is:

| | ✓ |
|---|---|
| £3,750 | ✓ |
| £3,500 | |
| £7,000 | |
| £7,250 | |

| | £ |
|---|---|
| Deemed proceeds of sale | 6,000 |
| Less disposal costs (10% × £2,500) | (250) |
| Net proceeds of sale | 5,750 |
| Less cost | (9,500) |
| Allowable loss | (3,750) |

The answer £3,500 does not deduct disposal costs. The answer £7,000 uses actual proceeds and does not deduct disposal costs. The answer £7,250 uses actual proceeds.

**(2)** A chattel with a useful life of 60 years or less is a wasting chattel.

| | ✓ |
|---|---|
| True | |
| False | ✓ |

A chattel with a useful life of 50 years or less is a wasting chattel.

- - - - - - - - - - - - - - - - - - - - - - - - - - - - - - - - - - - - - - - - - - - - - - - - - - - - - - - - - -

## Task 10 (10 marks)

### Share pool

| | No of shares | Cost £ |
|---|---|---|
| 14.4.01 Acquisition | 6,000 | 18,400 |
| 29.5.06 Rights 1 for 20 × £4 (1/20 × 6,000) | 300 | 1,200 |
| | 6,300 | 19,600 |
| 23.2.21 Disposal (3,500/6,300 × £19,600) | (3,500) | (10,889) |
| c/f | 2,800 | 8,711 |

### Total gain on sale

| | £ |
|---|---|
| First match with acquisitions in the next 30 days: | |
| Proceeds of sale $\frac{500}{4,000} \times £36,200$ | 4,525 |
| Less allowable cost | (3,400) |
| Gain | 1,125 |
| | |
| Next match with shares in the share pool: | |
| Proceeds of sale $\frac{3,500}{4,000} \times £36,200$ | 31,675 |
| Less allowable cost (from share pool above) | (10,889) |
| Gain | 20,786 |
| Total gains (£1,125 + £20,786) | 21,911 |

## Task 11 (7 marks)

**(a)**

| Explanation | Exempt (dates) | Chargeable (dates) |
|---|---|---|
| Actual occupation | 1 April 2005 to 30 September 2008 | |
| Four years employed elsewhere in UK | 1 October 2008 to 30 September 2012 | |
| Up to three years any reason | 1 October 2012 to 30 September 2013 | |
| Actual occupation | 1 October 2013 to 30 April 2014 | |
| Not occupied and not followed by actual occupation | | 1 May 2014 to 31 December 2019 |
| Last 9 months ownership | 1 January 2020 to 30 September 2020 | |

**(b)**

| | ✓ |
|---|---|
| True | |
| False | ✓ |

**(c)** Capital gains tax for 2020/21 is payable by:

| 31/01/2022 |
|---|

## Task 12 (6 marks)

**(a)** The chargeable estate for inheritance purposes is:

£    351,000

|  | £ |
| --- | --- |
| Cash to nephews £200 × 5 | 1,000 |
| ISA investments | 350,000 |
| Chargeable estate | 351,000 |

The small gifts exemption only applies to lifetime transfers. The ISA exemption only applies for income tax and capital gains tax. The residue to the wife is covered by the spouse exemption.

**(b)**

|  | ✓ |
| --- | --- |
| £170,000 |  |
| £88,000 |  |
| £136,000 | ✓ |
| £110,000 |  |

| | |
| --- | --- |
| 10.7.17 PET now chargeable | 600,000 |
| Less nil rate band available £(£325,000 – 150,000) | (175,000) |
|  | 425,000 |
| IHT @ 40% | 170,000 |
| Less taper relief (3 to 4 years) @ 20% | (34,000) |
| Death tax payable on lifetime transfer | 136,000 |

The chargeable lifetime transfer on 15 September 2012 is cumulated with the later PET since it was made in the seven years before that transfer.

The answer £170,000 does not include taper relief. The answer £88,000 deducts the full NRB. The answer £110,000 deducts the full NRB and does not include taper relief.

## Task 13 (6 marks)

**(a)**

| | ✓ |
|---|---|
| £3,000 | |
| £8,500 | ✓ |
| £6,000 | |
| £11,000 | |

| | £ |
|---|---|
| Marriage exemption (remoter ancestor) | 2,500 |
| Annual exemption 2019/20 | 3,000 |
| Annual exemption 2018/19 b/f | 3,000 |
| | 8,500 |

The answer £3,000 is the annual exemption for 2019/20 only. The answer £6,000 ignores the marriage exemption. The answer £11,000 uses the marriage exemption for immediate children.

**(b)**

| | ✓ |
|---|---|
| £55,000 | ✓ |
| £4,000 | |
| £6,000 | |
| £1,000 | |

| | £ |
|---|---|
| Before the gift: 5,100 shares × £30 | 153,000 |
| After the gift: 4,900 shares × £20 | (98,000) |
| Diminution in value | 55,000 |

The answer £4,000 is 200 shares at £20. The answer £6,000 is 200 shares at £30. The answer £1,000 is 200 shares at £5.

**(c)**

| £ | 118,750 |
|---|---|

| | £ |
|---|---|
| Net transfer of value (Jimmy pays IHT) | 800,000 |
| | |
| IHT    £325,000 × 0% = | Nil |
| £475,000 × 20/80 = | 118,750 |
| £800,000 | 118,750 |

BPP
LEARNING MEDIA

# BPP PRACTICE ASSESSMENT 4
# PERSONAL TAX

**Time allowed: 2.5 hours**

# Personal Tax (PLTX)
## BPP practice assessment 4

In the live assessment you will have access to the tax tables and reference material which have been reproduced at the back of this Question Bank. Please use them while completing this practice assessment so that you are familiar with their content.

## Task 1

In October 2017 her employer provided Antonia with a second-hand Ford Focus car. It cost the company £14,000, but the list price of this car when bought new was £21,000. The car has a $CO_2$ emission of 74 g/km, and has a petrol engine. The company sold the Ford Focus on 31 December 2020 and immediately provided Antonia with a brand new Volvo car (registered in December 2020). The Volvo has a list price of £27,000, but Antonia had to make a capital contribution of £6,500 towards it. The car has a $CO_2$ emission of 161g/km and has a diesel engine which does not meet the RDE2 standards.

The company pays for all running costs for both cars including the fuel. Antonia pays £80 per month to the company as a contribution towards the running costs of the cars.

(a) **The cost of the Ford Focus in the taxable benefit computation is:**

£ 

(b) **The taxable benefit in respect of the provision of the Ford Focus for private use in 2020/21 is:**

£ 

(c) **The taxable benefit in respect of the provision of fuel for the Ford Focus for private use in 2020/21 is:**

£ 

(d) **The cost of the Volvo in the taxable benefit computation is:**

£ 

(e) **The taxable benefit in respect of the provision of the Volvo for private use in 2020/21 is:**

£ 

(f) **The taxable benefit in respect of the provision of fuel for the Volvo for private use in 2020/21 is:**

£

## Task 2

**(a)** Elizabeth's employer provided her with a television for her private use on 6 April 2020, costing £2,500. Elizabeth did not pay anything for the use of the TV.

**(1)** **The taxable benefit for 2020/21 is:**

£ 

Elizabeth buys the TV from her employer for £750 on 5 April 2021, when it is worth £1,875.

**(2)** **The taxable benefit for 2020/21 is:**

£ 

**(b)** **Indicate whether the following benefits would be taxable or exempt if provided in 2020/21, by ticking the boxes:**

| Item | Taxable | Exempt |
|------|---------|--------|
| Provision of second mobile phone | | |
| Removal costs of £7,500 | | |
| Provision of parking space at work | | |
| Accommodation provided to a caretaker for proper performance of his employment duties | | |
| Membership of fitness club | | |

## Task 3

**(a)** **Millie is employed by RST plc. For each of the following payments, state the amount of employment income taxable in 2020/21. If an amount is not taxable in 2020/21 enter 0.**

**(1)** Monthly salary of £2,000. Millie becomes entitled to each month's salary on the 25th of each month and it is paid to her on the 28th of each month. Due to a bank error, the salary for March 2020 was not paid to her until 10 April 2020.

**The employment income for 2020/21 is:**

£ [                    ]

**(2)** Commission of £1,200 paid with her April 2021 salary. The commission relates to sales made in the month of March 2021 and is calculated once sales figures are finalised after month-end.

**The employment income for 2020/21 is:**

£ [                    ]

**(3)** Bonus of £5,000 paid on 30 April 2020 based on company's accounting profit for the year ended 31 December 2019 and calculated once profits are finalised.

**The employment income for 2020/21 is:**

£ [                    ]

**(4)** Reimbursement of business expenses of £500 in December 2020.

**The employment income for 2020/21 is:**

£ [                    ]

**(b)** In 2020/21, Calum had the following income:

Salary                                £47,900
Building society interest            £180
Dividends                            £100

Calum made a contribution of £2,500 to his employer's occupational pension scheme each year.

Using the proforma layout provided, prepare a computation of taxable income for 2020/21, clearly showing the distinction between the different types of income. Both brackets and minus signs can be used to show negative numbers.

| | Non-savings income £ | Savings income £ | Dividend income £ | Total £ |
|---|---|---|---|---|
| | | | | |
| | | | | |
| | | | | |
| | | | | |
| | | | | |
| | | | | |
| | | | | |
| | | | | |
| | | | | |

## Task 4

**(a)** Jim, an additional rate taxpayer, received £10,000 of bank interest and £5,500 of dividends during 2020/21. Of these amounts, £500 of interest and £300 of dividends were from his ISA accounts.

   **(1)** **Calculate the amount of interest on which Jim will pay income tax at a rate greater than 0% in 2020/21.**

     £ [        ]

   **(2)** **Calculate the amount of dividends on which Jim will pay income tax at a rate greater than 0% in 2020/21.**

     £ [        ]

**(b)** Myrtle has the following income for 2020/21: pension income of £105,000, bank interest of £4,800 and dividends of £3,600. She made net contributions of £2,400 to her personal pension scheme during 2020/21.

**(1)** **Myrtle's adjusted net income for 2020/21 is:**

£

**(2)** **Myrtle's taxable income for 2020/21 is:**

£

## Task 5

**(a)** **Is the following statement true or false?**

A taxpayer can choose between deducting the actual expenses incurred in letting their properties or claiming a £1,000 allowance per property per tax year.

| | ✔ |
|---|---|
| True | |
| False | |

**(b)** Zhu Liu bought an apartment on 1 October 2020. He let it out, unfurnished, from 1 December 2020 at an annual rent of £18,000 payable quarterly in advance. He incurred the following expenses in relation to the property:

| | £ |
|---|---|
| General repairs and maintenance, all incurred prior to 5 April 2021 | 750 |
| Insurance for the 12-month period ended 30 September 2021 paid on 1 October 2020 | 300 |
| Decorating paid for on 31 March 2021, for work carried out on 10 April 2021 | 500 |
| Installing a shower | 1,500 |

Using the proforma layout provided, calculate the property income for 2020/21. Fill in all the unshaded boxes. If an expense is not allowable, enter 0. Both brackets and minus signs can be used to show negative numbers.

| | £ |
|---|---|
| Rental income | |
| Repairs | |
| Insurance | |
| Decorating | |
| Shower | |
| Property income | |

## Task 6

**(a)** Denise works for Jules Ltd. She provides you with the following information:

(1) Annual salary £104,000 received on 25th day of each month.

(2) Employer's contribution of 5% of salary on 31 December 2020 to company's occupational pension scheme. Denise contributes 4% of her salary into this scheme.

(3) Bonus of £1,000 received 30 April 2020 based on company's accounting profit for the year ended 31 December 2019.

(4) Bonus of £1,200 received 30 April 2021 based on company's accounting profit for the year ended 31 December 2020.

(5) She has use of a company car for which the benefit in kind has been computed as £3,000. Denise pays for all the private petrol that she uses in this car.

(6) During 2020/21 Denise received £150 of bank interest and £50 of dividends from an ISA.

**Complete the following table showing the figures that should be included in Denise's taxable income for 2020/21. You should use whole pounds only. If your answer is zero, please input a '0'. If a number needs to be deducted please use either brackets or minus signs.**

|  | £ |
|---|---|
| Salary |  |
| Employer's pension contribution |  |
| Employee's pension contribution |  |
| Bonus received 30 April 2020 |  |
| Bonus received 30 April 2021 |  |
| Benefit in kind for car |  |
| Interest from bank |  |
| Dividends from ISA |  |
| Total income |  |
| Personal allowance |  |
| Taxable income |  |

**(b)** Denise's brother has net income of £72,000. Calculate his income tax liability for 2020/21

|  |  |
|---|---|
|  |  |
|  |  |
|  |  |
|  |  |

## Task 7

**(a)** A client has told you that she forgot to include some bank interest in the tax return you prepared, and she does not intend to tell HMRC of the omission.

**What TWO actions should you take?**

| | ✓ |
|---|---|
| Inform the Association of Accounting Technicians about the omission | |
| Report the client's refusal and the facts surrounding it to your firm's Money Laundering Reporting Officer | |
| Inform the client in writing that it is not possible for you to act for her in connection with that return | |
| Inform HMRC about the omission | |

**(b)** Mike is wishing to sell several assets in 2020/21 and the gains will be more than his annual exemption. He has £3,000 left of his basic rate band. His civil partner, Rob, will not be using his annual exemption this year and is a basic rate taxpayer.

**What advice would you give your client in order to minimise his tax liability on the sale of the assets.**

## Task 8

**(a)** **Which TWO of the following statements are true about inheritance tax?**

(1)   It is an indirect tax.
(2)   It is a progressive tax.
(3)   It is an environmental tax.
(4)   It is a direct tax.

|  | ✓ |
|---|---|
| 1 and 3 |  |
| 1 and 4 |  |
| 2 and 3 |  |
| 2 and 4 |  |

**(b)** **Which TWO of the following statements concerning tax evasion and tax avoidance are correct?**

|  | ✓ |
|---|---|
| Tax evasion is illegal |  |
| Both tax evasion and tax avoidance are illegal |  |
| Tax avoidance involves any legal method of reducing the taxpayer's tax burden |  |
| Tax evasion always involves providing HM Revenue & Customs with false information |  |

**(c)** **Which TWO of the following statements are correct about how your firm should deal with the suggestion from a client that no disclosure is made to HMRC of their capital gain?**

|  | ✓ |
|---|---|
| The client should be advised to disclose details of the capital gain to HMRC |  |
| If the client does not disclose the gain to HMRC, your firm can definitely still continue to act for him |  |
| If your firm ceases to act for to client, it must disclose this to HMRC and provide detailed reasons why it has ceased to act |  |
| If the client does not disclose the gain to HMRC, your firm would be obliged to report under the money laundering regulations. |  |

# Task 9

**(a)** **Classify whether a disposal of each of the following assets will be chargeable to or exempt from capital gains tax:**

| Asset | Chargeable | Exempt |
|---|---|---|
| Plot of land sold for £20,000 | | |
| Diamond brooch sold for £3,500 which cost £2,000 | | |
| Shares in an unlisted company sold for £10,000 | | |
| 1930 Rolls Royce car sold for £100,000 | | |

**(b)** Jaycee made the following gains and loss in 2020/21:

| | £ |
|---|---|
| Gain on shares September 2020 | 18,500 |
| Gain on painting December 2020 | 6,600 |
| Gain on statue January 2021 | 18,895 |
| Loss on vase 8 April 2020 | (9,700) |

Jaycee is a higher rate taxpayer.

**(1)** **Her capital gains tax liability for 2020/21 is:**

£ [ ]

**(2)** **The due date for payment of this liability is: (enter date as xx/xx/xxxx)**

[ ]

**(c)** In December 2020, Mabel gave her son an asset worth £20,000. She had acquired the asset for £25,000.

In March 2021, Mabel gave her sister an asset worth £30,000. Mabel had acquired the asset for £22,000.

**Mabel's chargeable gains (before the annual exempt amount) for 2020/21 are:**

£ [ ]

## Task 10

**(a)** Ming Lee bought 1,000 shares in Lavender Ltd for £5,000 in October 2005. In May 2007, she received 200 shares in a bonus issue. In January 2011 the company offered a rights issue at 1 share for every 6 held. She accepted this rights issue at £3 per share. In November 2018 she purchased 2,000 for £12,000. She sold 1,000 shares in Lavender Ltd in January 2021 for £12,400.

**Clearly showing the balance of shares and their value to carry forward, calculate the chargeable gain on sale of the shares. All workings must be shown.**

| | | |
|---|---|---|
| Proceeds | 12,400 | |
| Cost (Pool) | 5,176 | |
| Gain | 7,224 | |
| | | |
| | | |
| Oct 2005 Purchase | 1000 | 5000 |
| May 2007 Bonus | 200 | — |
| | 1200 | 5000 |
| Jan 2011 Rights 1/6 @3 | 200 | 600 |
| | 1400 | 5600 |
| Nov 2018 Pur | 2000 | 12000 |
| | 3400 | 17,600 |
| Sale (1000/3,400) x 17,600 | 1000 | (5,176) |
| c/f | 2400 | 12,424 |

**(b)** In 2020/21 Yen sold an antique watch for £8,000 which he had bought in 2015 for £4,000.

Yen's chargeable gain in 2020/21 will be:

| | ✓ |
|---|---|
| £4,000 | |
| £3,333 | ✓ |
| £0 | |
| £2,000 | |

*Calculate the Gain as normal do const exceed 5/3*

*LVP?*

........................................................................................

# Task 11

**(a)** On 1 March 2000, Craig bought a house for £36,000. He had lived in it until 1 September 2003, when he went to Australia to take up employment. He returned from there on 1 September 2009 and moved back into the house until 1 November 2015 when he purchased a small flat. He has lived in the flat since then. Craig finally sold the house for £178,000 on 31 October 2020.

**Using the proforma layout below, show the chargeable gain on sale. Both brackets and minus signs can be used to show negative numbers.**

| Chargeable gain on sale of property | £ |
|---|---|
| Proceeds of sale | |
| Less allowable cost | |
| Gain before PRR | |
| Less PRR exempt amount | |
| Chargeable gain | |

**(b)** During 2020/21 Nina has sold an asset giving rise to a chargeable gain of £21,000. She has capital losses brought forward at 6 April 2020 of £11,000.

**The amount of capital losses Nina will have to carry forward at 5 April 2021 is:**

|  | ✓ |
|---|---|
| £2,300 | |
| £0 | |
| £11,000 | |
| £8,700 | |

## Task 12

Ada died on 25 April 2020. Her death estate was valued at £623,000. Her executors paid funeral expenses of £3,000 on 12 May 2020. Under the terms of her will Ada left £150,000 to her husband, a specific legacy of £40,000 to her sister, and the residue of the estate to her children. She has no nil band available on death and did not own any property.

**(a)  How much inheritance tax would be due on her death estate?**

|  | ✓ |
|---|---|
| £172,000 | |
| £58,000 | |
| £248,000 | |
| £188,000 | |

**(b)  When would the IHT be due on her death estate?**

|  | ✓ |
|---|---|
| 31/01/2021 | |
| 31/10/20 | |
| 30/04/21 | |
| 05/04/21 | |

## Task 13

Afiya died on 29 November 2020. She had made the following gifts during her lifetime:

(1) On 14 September 2018, Afiya made a gift of 6,500 £1 ordinary shares in Cassava Ltd, an unquoted investment company, to her daughter.

Before the transfer Afiya owned 8,000 shares out of Cassava Ltd's issued share capital of 10,000 £1 ordinary shares. On 14 September 2018, Cassava Ltd's shares were worth £3 each for a holding of 15%, £7 each for a holding of 65%, and £8 each for a holding of 80%.

(2) On 27 January 2019, Afiya made a cash gift of £400,000 to a trust. Afiya paid the inheritance tax arising from this gift.

**Calculate the lifetime tax paid, and the death tax arising on these gifts as a result of her death.**

This style of question would be human marked in the exam.

Value of shares b/a        8000 × 8 = 64,000
Value of share after       1500 × 3 = (4,500)

Transfer of value                      59,500
Less (AE 2019/2020)                    (3,000)
    (AE 2020/2021)                     (3,000)

PRT                                     53,500

# BPP PRACTICE ASSESSMENT 4
# PERSONAL TAX

## ANSWERS

# Personal Tax (PLTX)
# BPP practice assessment 4

## Task 1

**(a)** The cost of the Ford Focus in the taxable benefit computation is:

| £ | 21,000 |
|---|--------|

**(b)** The taxable benefit in respect of the provision of the Ford Focus for private use in 2020/21 is:

| £ | 2,273 |
|---|-------|

£21,000 × 19% × 9/12 – (£80 × 9) = £2,273

14% + (70 – 55)/5% + 2% (pre-April 2020) = 19%

**(c)** The taxable benefit in respect of the provision of fuel for the Ford Focus for private use in 2020/21 is:

| £ | 3,491 |
|---|-------|

£24,500 × 19% × 9/12

**(d)** The cost of the Volvo in the taxable benefit computation is:

| £ | 22,000 |
|---|--------|

£27,000 – £5,000 (max deduction for capital contribution)

**(e)** The taxable benefit in respect of the provision of the Volvo for private use in 2020/21 is:

| £ | 1,795 |
|---|-------|

£22,000 × 37% × 3/12 – (£80 × 3) = £1,795
14% + (160 – 55)/5% + 4% (diesel) = 39% capped at 37%

**(f)** The taxable benefit in respect of the provision of fuel for the Volvo for private use in 2020/21 is:

| £ | 2,266 |
|---|-------|

£24,500 × 37% × 3/12

BPP
LEARNING MEDIA

# Task 2

**(a)** **(1)** The taxable benefit for 2020/21 is:

| £ | 500 |
|---|-----|

Use of asset £2,500 × 20%

**(2)** The taxable benefit for 2020/21 is:

| £ | 1,250 |
|---|-------|

Greater of:

| | | £ |
|---|---|---|
| (i) | Original market value | 2,500 |
| | Less assessed for use 2020/21 | (500) |
| | | 2,000 |
| (ii) | Market value at acquisition by employee | 1,875 |

Greater = £2,000 less amount paid by Elizabeth of £750

**(b)**

| Item | Taxable | Exempt |
|------|:-------:|:------:|
| Provision of second mobile phone | ✓ | |
| Removal costs of £7,500 | | ✓ |
| Provision of parking space at work | | ✓ |
| Accommodation provided to a caretaker for proper performance of his employment duties | | ✓ |
| Membership of fitness club | ✓ | |

## Task 3

**(a)** **(1)** The employment income for 2020/21 is:

£ | 24,000

April 2020 to March 2021 = 12 × £2,000

The salary for March 2020 was received for tax purposes on 25 March 2020 when Millie became entitled to it and so was taxed in 2019/20.

**(2)** The employment income for 2020/21 is:

£ | 0

Commission received 25 April 2021 (taxed in 2021/22)

**(3)** The employment income for 2020/21 is:

£ | 5,000

Bonus received 30 April 2020

**(4)** The employment income for 2020/21 is:

£ | 0

This is exempt as the reimbursement is covered by an allowable deduction.

**(b)**

| | Non-savings income £ | Savings income £ | Dividend income £ | Total £ |
|---|---|---|---|---|
| Employment income: | | | | |
| Salary | 47,900 | | | |
| Less occupational pension contribution | (2,500) | | | |
| Employment income | 45,400 | | | |
| Building society interest | | 180 | | |
| Dividends | | | 100 | |
| Net income | 45,400 | 180 | 100 | 45,680 |
| Less personal allowance | (12,500) | | | (12,500) |
| Taxable income | 32,900 | 180 | 100 | 33,180 |

## Task 4

**(a)** **(1)** The amount of interest on which Jim will pay income tax at a rate greater than 0% in 2020/21 is:

| £ | 9,500 |
|---|-------|

ISA interest is exempt. No savings allowance due.

**(2)** The amount of dividends on which Jim will pay income tax at a rate greater than 0% in 2020/21 is:

| £ | 3,200 |
|---|-------|

£5,500 – £2,000 dividend allowance – £300 ISA dividends (exempt)

**(b)** **(1)** Myrtle's adjusted net income for 2020/21 is:

| £ | 110,400 |
|---|---------|

|  | Total £ |
|--|---------|
| Pension income | 105,000 |
| Bank interest | 4,800 |
| Dividends | 3,600 |
| Total income | 113,400 |
| Less: pension contributions (£2,400 × 100/80) | (3,000) |
| Adjusted net income | 110,400 |

**(2)** Myrtle's taxable income (before the savings and dividend allowances) for 2020/21 is:

£ | 106,100

| | £ |
|---|---|
| Adjusted net income | 110,400 |
| Less income limit | (100,000) |
| Excess | 10,400 |
| | |
| Personal allowance | 12,500 |
| Less half excess | (5,200) |
| | 7,300 |

Taxable income is therefore: £113,400 – £7,300 = £106,100

# Task 5

**(a)**

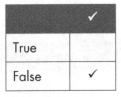

| | ✓ |
|---|---|
| True | |
| False | ✓ |

The £1,000 property allowance is per taxpayer, not per property.

**(b)**

| | £ |
|---|---|
| Rental income £18,000/4 × 2 (1 December and 1 March) | 9,000 |
| Repairs | (750) |
| Insurance £300 | (300) |
| Decorating (paid for in 2020/21)) | (500) |
| Shower (capital expense) | 0 |
| Property income | 7,450 |

## Task 6

### (a)

| | £ |
|---|---|
| Salary | 104,000 |
| Employer's pension contribution (exempt) | 0 |
| Employee's pension contribution (£104,000 × 4%) | (4,160) |
| Bonus received 30 April 2020 | 1,000 |
| Bonus received 30 April 2021 | 0 |
| Benefit in kind for car | 3,000 |
| Interest from bank | 150 |
| Dividends from ISA (exempt) | 0 |
| Total income | 103,990 |
| Personal allowance<br>£(12,500 – 1,995 ((103,990 – 100,000)/2)) | (10,505) |
| Taxable income | 93,485 |

### (b)

| | £ |
|---|---|
| Net income | 72,000 |
| Personal allowance | (12,500) |
| Taxable income | 59,500 |
| | |
| Tax: | |
| 37,500 × 20% | 7,500 |
| 22,000 × 40% | 8,800 |
| Income tax liability | 16,300 |

## Task 7

**(a)**

|  | ✓ |
|---|---|
| Inform the Association of Accounting Technicians about the omission |  |
| Report the client's refusal and the facts surrounding it to your firm's Money Laundering Reporting Officer | ✓ |
| Inform the client in writing that it is not possible for you to act for her in connection with that return | ✓ |
| Inform HMRC about the omission |  |

**(b)**

Transfers between civil partners are at no gain no loss and so Mike could transfer assets to Rob sufficient to make gains up to Rob's annual exemption.

If Mike is then left with gains of more than £15,300 (his annual exemption of £12,300 plus his unused basic rate band of £3,000) then he will have to consider transferring more to Rob so that the gains are taxed at the basic rate of 10% rather than the higher rate of 20%.

The issue with this is that the transfers have to be 'no strings attached' so Mike could not ask Rob for the net proceeds of these sales once all the transactions have taken place and the tax has been paid. This is something that Mike and Rob will have to discuss between them.

An alternative would be for Mike to delay the sale of some of the assets so that he has two annual exemptions available (2020/21 and 2021/22). This would enable Mike to retain the sale proceeds from those assets.

## Task 8

**(a)**

| | ✓ |
|---|---|
| 1 and 3 | |
| 1 and 4 | |
| 2 and 3 | |
| 2 and 4 | ✓ |

Inheritance tax is a progressive tax as the proportion of the wealth that is taxable increases as wealth increases (the amount covered by the nil rate band is charged at 0% and the remainder at 20% (in life) or 40% (on death)).

Inheritance tax is a direct tax as it is on a specific individual's wealth.

**(b)**

| | ✓ |
|---|---|
| Tax evasion is illegal | ✓ |
| Both tax evasion and tax avoidance are illegal | |
| Tax avoidance involves any legal method of reducing the taxpayer's tax burden | ✓ |
| Tax evasion always involves providing HM Revenue & Customs with false information | |

Tax evasion is illegal and Tax avoidance involves any legal method of reducing the taxpayer's tax burden.

Tax evasion does not necessarily involve providing HM Revenue & Customs (HMRC) with false information. It could include this situation where a taxpayer is evading tax by not providing HMRC with information to which it is entitled.

**(c)**

|  | ✓ |
|---|:---:|
| The client should be advised to disclose details of the capital gain to HMRC | ✓ |
| If the client does not disclose the gain to HMRC, your firm can definitely still continue to act for him | |
| If your firm ceases to act for to client, it must disclose this to HMRC and provide detailed reasons why it has ceased to act | |
| If the client does not disclose the gain to HMRC, your firm would be obliged to report under the money laundering regulations. | ✓ |

The client should be advised to disclose details of the capital gain to HMRC and if the client does not disclose the gain to HMRC, your firm would be obliged to report under the money laundering regulations.

Your firm should also consider ceasing to act for the client. If it does cease to act, your firm should notify HMRC that it no longer acts for him although your firm should not provide any reason for this.

························································································

## Task 9

**(a)**

| Asset | Chargeable | Exempt |
|---|:---:|:---:|
| Plot of land sold for £20,000 | ✓ | |
| Diamond brooch sold for £3,500 which cost £2,000 | | ✓<br>(Chattel – cost and proceeds no more than £6,000) |
| Shares in an unlisted company sold for £10,000 | ✓ | |
| 1930 Rolls Royce car sold for £100,000 | | ✓<br>(all cars exempt) |

**(b)** **(1)** Her capital gains tax liability for 2020/21 is:

£ | 4,399

| | £ |
|---|---|
| Gain on shares | 18,500 |
| Gain on painting | 6,600 |
| Gain on statue | 18,895 |
| Chargeable gains | 43,995 |
| Less allowable loss on vase | (9,700) |
| Net chargeable gains for year | 34,295 |
| Less annual exempt amount | (12,300) |
| Taxable gains | 21,995 |
| | |
| CGT: £21,995 × 20% (higher rate taxpayer) | 4,399 |

**(2)** The due date for payment of this liability is:

31/01/2022

**(c)** Mabel's chargeable gains (before the annual exempt amount) for 2020/21 are:

£ | 8,000

| | £ |
|---|---|
| Gift to her sister: | |
| Deemed proceeds of sale (market value) | 30,000 |
| Less allowable cost | (22,000) |
| Chargeable gain | 8,000 |

Both the son and the sister are connected persons for Mabel. However, the loss of £5,000 on the disposal to the son can only be set against gains made to him, not to another connected person.

........................................................................

## Task 10

### (a) Share pool

| | No of shares | Cost £ |
|---|---|---|
| October 2005 Acquisition | 1,000 | 5,000 |
| May 2007 Bonus | 200 | Nil |
| | 1,200 | 5,000 |
| January 2011 Rights 1 for 6 × £3 (1/6 × 1,200 = 200 shares × £3 = £600) | 200 | 600 |
| | 1,400 | 5,600 |
| November 2018 Acquisition | 2,000 | 12,000 |
| | 3,400 | 17,600 |
| January 2021 Disposal (1,000/3,400 × £17,600) | (1,000) | (5,176) |
| c/f | 2,400 | 12,424 |
| **Gain** | | |
| Proceeds of sale | | 12,400 |
| Less allowable cost | | (5,176) |
| Chargeable gain | | 7,224 |

### (b) Yen's chargeable gain in 2020/21 will be:

| | ✓ |
|---|---|
| £4,000 | |
| £3,333 | ✓ |
| £0 | |
| £2,000 | |

The actual gain of £4,000 (£8,000 − £4,000) is restricted to £3,333 (5/3 × (8,000 − £6,000)) under the chattel rules. The answer £4,000 is the actual gain. The answer £nil assumes an exempt disposal. The answer £2,000 restricts the proceeds to £6,000.

# Task 11

**(a)**

| Chargeable gain on sale of property | £ |
|---|---|
| Proceeds of sale | 178,000 |
| Less allowable cost | (36,000) |
| Gain before PRR | 142,000 |
| Less PRR exempt amount ((197/248) × 142,000) | (112,798) |
| Chargeable gain | 29,202 |

**Working**

| Time period | Chargeable months | Exempt months | Total months |
|---|---|---|---|
| 1.3.00 to 31.8.03 | | 42 | 42 |
| 1.9.03 to 31.8.09 (**Note. 1**) | | 72 | 72 |
| 1.9.09 to 31.10.15 | | 74 | 74 |
| 1.11.15 to 31.10.20 (**Note. 2**) | 51 | 9 | 60 |
| | 51 | 197 | 248 |

**Notes.**

1   Any period of employment abroad is treated as deemed occupation if it is preceded and followed by actual occupation.

2   Last nine months of ownership is always exempt if the property has been the taxpayer's only or main residence at some time during the ownership period.

**(b)** The amount of capital losses Nina will have to carry forward at 5 April 2021 is:

|         |   |
|---------|---|
| £2,300  | ✓ |
| £0      |   |
| £11,000 |   |
| £8,700  |   |

The capital loss brought forward will be used after the annual exempt amount. This uses £8,700 of the loss leaving £2,300 to carry forward to 2021/22. The answer £0 uses the losses brought forward before deducting the annual exempt amount. The answer £11,000 assumes none of the losses can be carried forward. The answer £8,700 is the amount of losses used.

# Task 12

**(a)**

|          |   |
|----------|---|
| £172,000 |   |
| £58,000  |   |
| £248,000 |   |
| £188,000 | ✓ |

**Death estate**

|                                      | £         |
|--------------------------------------|-----------|
| Assets at death                      | 623,000   |
| Less funeral expenses                | (3,000)   |
| Value of estate for IHT purposes     | 620,000   |
| Less exempt legacy to spouse         | (150,000) |
| Chargeable estate                    | 470,000   |
|                                      |           |
| IHT liability £470,000 × 40%         | 188,000   |

BPP
LEARNING MEDIA

The answer £172,000 treats the legacy to her sister as exempt from IHT. The answer £58,000 deducts the nil rate band. The answer £248,000 ignores the exempt legacy to spouse.

**(b)**

|  | ✓ |
|---|---|
| 31/01/2021 |  |
| 31/10/20 | ✓ |
| 30/04/21 |  |
| 05/04/21 |  |

Six months from the end of the month of death.

........................................................................

## Task 13

### Lifetime transfers

14 September 2018:

|  | £ |
|---|---|
| Value of shares held before transfer 8,000 × £8 | 64,000 |
| Less value of shares held after transfer 1,500 × £3 | (4,500) |
| Transfer of value | 59,500 |
| Less: annual exemption 2018/19 | (3,000) |
| annual exemption 2017/18 b/f | (3,000) |
| Potentially exempt transfer | 53,500 |

27 January 2019:

|  | £ |
|---|---|
| Net chargeable transfer | 400,000 |
| Annual exemptions applied to PET | |
| **IHT** | |
| 325,000 × 0% | 0 |
| 75,000 × 20/80 (donor pays tax) | 18,750 |
| 400,000 | 18,750 |
| | |
| Gross chargeable transfer £(400,000 + 18,750) | 418,750 |

## Additional tax on lifetime transfer on death of donor

14 September 2018:

Potentially exempt transfer of £53,500 becomes chargeable as donor dies within seven years.

Within nil rate band at death, no tax to pay.

27 January 2018:

Nil rate band available £(325,000 − 53,500) = £271,500.

|  | £ |
|---|---|
| Gross chargeable transfer | 418,750 |
| | |
| **IHT** | |
| 271,500 × 0% | 0 |
| 147,250 × 40% | 58,900 |
| 418,750 | 58,900 |
| No taper relief (death within three years of transfer) | |
| Less lifetime tax paid | (18,750) |
| Additional tax payable on death | 40,150 |

# BPP PRACTICE ASSESSMENT 5
# PERSONAL TAX

**Time allowed: 2.5 hours**

# Personal Tax (PLTX)
# BPP practice assessment 5

In the live assessment you will have access to the tax tables and reference material which have been reproduced at the back of this Question Bank. Please use them while completing this practice assessment so that you are familiar with their content.

## Task 1

**(a)** You are a sole practitioner and suspect that one of your clients may be engaged in money laundering.

**Who should you inform about your suspicions?**

|  | ✓ |
| --- | --- |
| National Crime Agency |  |
| Association of Taxation Technicians |  |
| Tax Tribunal |  |
| HM Treasury |  |

**(b)** On 30 September 2021 your client, Jakki, leaves the following message on your voicemail:

'Hi, it's Jakki. I know that I am a new client to your practice and that you did not prepare my tax return for 2020/21, but I have just discovered that I failed to notify HMRC of some dividends that I received in January 2020. I simply forgot about them, but I am worried that HMRC will find out that I have not paid the right amount of tax on this income. Can you please advise about what I should do? Thanks.'

**List the information that you need to give Jakki when you ring her back to discuss this issue.**

## Task 2

**(a)** Yan is provided with a company car for business and private use throughout 2020/21. The car had a list price of £17,200 when bought new in December 2019, although the company paid £16,000 for the car after a dealer discount. Yan made a contribution of £2,000 towards the cost of the car.

The car has a petrol engine and has $CO_2$ emissions of 87g/km. The company pays for all running costs, including all fuel. Yan does not make any contribution for his private use of the car.

**(1) The cost of the car in the taxable benefit computation is:**

£ [                    ]

**(2) The percentage used in the taxable benefit computation is:**

[                    ] %

**(3) The taxable benefit in respect of the provision of fuel for private use is:**

£ [                    ]

**(b)** You have received the following email from Matt Taylor:

| | |
|---|---|
| **From:** | MTaylor@boxmail.net |
| **To:** | AATStudent@boxmail.net |
| **Sent:** | 14 June 2021 11:35 |
| **Subject:** | Car |

I have recently been promoted and now have to do some travelling by car on business, probably about 6,000 miles a year. My employer has given me two options:

(1) A brand new company car with a list price of £15,000. It has a petrol engine. The car is environmentally friendly and so has $CO_2$ emissions of only 53g/km. I will be able to use the car for both business and private purposes, but I will be required to repay the cost of my private fuel.

(2) A mileage allowance of 35p per business mile if I use my own car.

Can you please explain the taxation aspects of each of the options?

Thanks, Matt

**Reply to Matt's email**

| | |
|---|---|
| **From:** | AATStudent@boxmail.net |
| **To:** | MTaylor@boxmail.net |
| **Sent:** | 16 June 2021 10:41 |
| **Subject:** | Car |

..........................................................................................

## Task 3

**(a)** **(1)** Marge works for LMN plc. She was given a staff suggestion scheme bonus of £7,000 for recommending a senior member of staff.

**The taxable benefit for 2020/21 is:**

| £ | |
|---|---|

**(2)** **Tick to show if the following statement is true or false.**

The maximum amount of exempt benefit for the additional costs of home working is £6 per week.

| | ✓ |
|---|---|
| True | |
| False | |

**(b)** For each of the following benefits, tick whether they would be wholly or partly taxable or wholly exempt if received in 2020/21:

| Item | Wholly or partly taxable | Wholly exempt |
|---|---|---|
| Mobile phone | | |
| Removal expenses of £9,000 | | |
| Incidental personal expenses of working away from home in the UK of £10 per night | | |
| Staff party at cost of £100 per head | | |

**(c)** Antonia is employed by Zed Ltd. She receives store vouchers from the company as a Christmas bonus in December 2020. These enable her to buy goods worth £300. Her employer bought the vouchers from the store for £267.

**(1)** The taxable benefit for 2020/21 is:

£ [          ]

Antonia is also loaned £12,000 by Zed Ltd on 1 July 2020. She pays interest at an annual rate of 0.5% on the loan. She does not make any capital repayments in 2020/21.

**(2)** The taxable benefit for 2020/21 is:

£ [          ]

# Task 4

**(a)** During 2020/21, Mimi received the following income. In each case, show the amount of income that she should enter on her tax return. If the income is exempt, enter 0.

**(1)** Property income £2,000.

£ [          ]

**(2)** Premium bond prize £100.

£ [          ]

**(3)** **Government stock interest £80.**

£ ☐

**(4)** **Dividends received from an ISA of £2,000.**

£ ☐

**(b)** Marcello receives a dividend of £5,400 in March 2021. He is an additional rate taxpayer.

**(1)** **The amount of the dividend that Marcello will pay income tax on at a rate greater than 0% is:**

£ ☐

**(2)** **The tax payable on the dividend is:**

£ ☐

**(3)** Marcello also has some building society interest.

**Is the following statement true or false?**

Marcello will pay tax at 0% on the first £500 of this interest.

| | ✓ |
|-------|---|
| True | |
| False | |

## Task 5

**(a)** Ronnie buys a house on 6 May 2020 and rents it out on 6 August 2020. He charges an annual rent of £9,000, payable in advance. He pays an annual insurance premium on 6 June 2020 of £600. He has chosen to use the accruals basis to calculate his property profits.

**Ronnie's taxable property income for 2020/21 is:**

£ ☐

**(b)** A client, Mohamed Albayouk, has sent in the following information for 2020/21 in relation to his two properties that he rents out.

17 Wool Lane is unfurnished and is rented out at £560 per month. 42 Silk Street is furnished and is rented out at £800 per month. Both properties were occupied throughout 2020/21.

The expenses for the year were:

| Item | 17 Wool Lane £ | 42 Silk Street £ |
|---|---|---|
| Insurance | 300 | 280 |
| Water rates | 160 | 176 |
| Council tax | 1,800 | 2,100 |
| Cleaning | 800 | 500 |
| New en-suite (Note 1) | 4,000 | 0 |
| Cost of replacement furniture (Note 2) | 0 | 3,450 |

**Note 1: The en-suite was newly installed in what had previously been storage space.**

**Note: Included in the replacement furniture is a combination oven-microwave costing £700. This replaced a basic microwave which would have cost £150.**

**Calculate the property income taxable on Mohamed Albayouk for 2020/21 using the proforma layout provided. Fill in all the unshaded boxes. If any item is not an allowable expense, enter 0. Both brackets and minus signs can be used to show negative numbers.**

| | 17 Wool Lane £ | 42 Silk Street £ |
|---|---|---|
| Income: | | |
| Rents | | |
| Expenses: | | |
| Insurance | | |
| Water rates | | |
| Council tax | | |
| Cleaning | | |
| Redecoration | | |
| Replacement furniture relief | | |
| Property income | | |
| Total property income | | |

**(c)** Asif owns three properties which he lets out throughout 2020/21. He makes a profit of £5,000 on Property 1, a loss of £1,200 on Property 2 and a profit of £2,000 on Property 3. Asif also has a property loss of £1,500 brought forward at 5 April 2020.

**The property income taxable on Asif for 2020/21 is:**

| £ | |
|---|---|

## Task 6

Andrew has income as follows:

| | £ |
|---|---|
| Employment income | 58,850 |
| Bank interest received | 1,600 |
| Dividends received | 9,500 |

Andrew makes a Gift Aid donation of £1,200 in July 2020.

**Calculate his total income tax liability for 2020/21, using the table given below. Both brackets and minus signs can be used to show negative numbers.**

| | £ |
|---|---|
| | |
| | |
| | |
| | |
| | |
| | |
| | |
| | |
| | |
| | |
| | |
| | |

| | £ |
|---|---|
| | |
| | |
| | |

......................................................................................

## Task 7

**(a)  Which of the following taxpayers is UK resident for the tax year 2020/21 on the basis of the information given?**

    (1)    Suzy, previously UK resident, present in UK between 6 April 2020 and 5 December 2021

    (2)    Miles, not previously UK resident, present in UK between 6 April 2020 and 5 May 2020

| | ✓ |
|---|---|
| 1 and 2 | |
| 1 only | |
| 2 only | |
| Neither 1 nor 2 | |

**(b)  Which TWO of the following types of income are exempt from income tax?**

    (1)    Interest on an NS&I Investment account
    (2)    Premium bond prizes
    (3)    Interest on UK Government stocks ('gilts')
    (4)    Dividends on shares held in an Individual Savings Account

| | ✓ |
|---|---|
| 1 and 2 | |
| 1 and 4 | |
| 2 and 3 | |
| 2 and 4 | |

**(c)** Sarah has a salary of £46,000. She also has the use of a company car with a taxable benefit if £3,850.

**What national insurance contributions are suffered by Sarah and her employer? Give your answers to the nearest penny.**

**Class 1 Employee**

£

**Class 1 Employer**

£

**Class 1A**

£

## Task 8

Gavin is employed by XYZ plc.

**For each of the following payments, state the amount of employment income taxable in 2020/21. If an amount is not taxable in 2020/21 enter 0.**

**(a)** Annual salary received in monthly payments on the last working day of each month. Until the end of December 2020, his annual salary was £36,000. He had a 2% annual pay increase with effect from 1 January 2021.

**The salary to be included in employment income for 2020/21 is:**

£

**(b)** Bonus of £2,000 received 31 March 2021 based on company's accounting profit for the year ended 31 December 2020.

**The bonus to be included in employment income for 2020/21 is:**

£

**(c)** Commission of £500 received 30 April 2021 on sales made in the month of March 2021.

**The commission to be included in employment income for 2020/21 is:**

£

**(d)** Employer's contribution of £5,000 on 10 March 2021 towards Gavin's occupational pension scheme.

**The benefit to be included in employment income for 2020/21 is:**

| £ | |
|---|---|

## Task 9

**(a)** **For each of the following assets, tick whether they are chargeable or exempt assets for capital gains tax:**

| Asset | Chargeable | Exempt |
|---|---|---|
| Horse | | |
| Field in which horse is kept | | |
| Antique horse brass costing £500, worth £1,700 | | |

**(b)** Ulma bought a holiday cottage for £65,000 and spent £15,000 on an extension and £10,000 on redecoration. She sold the cottage for £125,000 on 10 August 2020.

**The chargeable gain on sale is:**

| £ | |
|---|---|

**(c)** Jade purchased an emerald bracelet for £8,000. She sold the bracelet in August 2020 at auction for £2,700 (which was net of 10% commission).

**The allowable loss on sale is:**

| £ | |
|---|---|

**(d)** Lionel sold 2 acres of land in September 2020 for £125,000. The original 10 acres had cost him £70,000 in June 2001. The remaining 8 acres had a market value of £375,000 at the date of sale.

The chargeable gain on sale is:

| £ | |
|---|---|

## Task 10

Merrill paid £5,000 for 2,000 shares in Bug plc in August 2009. In September 2012, there was a one for one bonus issue. In October 2014 Merrill purchased a further 1,000 shares for £7,000 and in November 2016 there was a 3 for 2 rights issue at £6 per share. Merrill sold 1,000 shares in June 2020 for £8,000.

**Compute the chargeable gain and the value of the share pool following the disposal, using the proforma layout provided. Both brackets and minus signs can be used to show negative numbers.**

**Gain**

|  | £ |
|---|---|
|  |  |
|  |  |
|  |  |
|  |  |

**Share pool**

|  | No of shares | Cost £ |
|---|---|---|
|  |  |  |
|  |  |  |
|  |  |  |
|  |  |  |
|  |  |  |
|  |  |  |
|  |  |  |
|  |  |  |
|  |  |  |

# Task 11

**(a)** Jai makes chargeable gains (on antiques) of £17,000 in November 2020. Jai's taxable income for 2020/21 is £36,890 and he made a Gift Aid payment of £400 to Oxfam in May 2020. Jai has a loss brought forward from 2019/20 of £1,000.

**The CGT payable for 2020/21 is:**

| £ |   |
|---|---|
|   |   |

**(b)** **Tick to show if the following statement is true or false.**

The last nine months of ownership of a house are exempt provided that the house is lived in by the owner at some time during that nine-month period.

|       | ✓ |
|-------|---|
| True  |   |
| False |   |

---

# Task 12

**(a)** On 7 July 2016, Paul made a gross chargeable transfer (after all exemptions) of £260,000. On 19 December 2020 he gave £190,000 to a trust. Paul agreed to pay any lifetime IHT due. Paul has not made any other chargeable lifetime transfers in recent years.

**How much inheritance tax will be payable by Paul on the December 2020 transfer of value?**

|         | ✓ |
|---------|---|
| £0      |   |
| £31,250 |   |
| £29,750 |   |
| £23,800 |   |

**(b)** Dan owned all 1,000 shares in Z Ltd, an unquoted investment company. On 10 October 2020, Dan gave 300 of his shares in Z Ltd to his daughter. The values of the shares on 10 October 2020 were as follows:

| % shareholding | Value per share £ |
|---|---|
| 76 – 100 | 150 |
| 51 – 75 | 120 |
| 26 – 50 | 90 |
| 1 – 25 | 30 |

**What is the diminution in value of Dan's estate as a result of his gift on 10 October 2019?**

| | ✓ |
|---|---|
| £84,000 | |
| £27,000 | |
| £66,000 | |
| £45,000 | |

**(c)** Susanna died on 19 November 2020. Her estate consisted of a house worth £245,000 (on which there was a repayment mortgage of £60,000) and investments and cash totalling £455,000. Her executors paid funeral expenses of £5,000. Susanna left a cash legacy of £100,000 to her husband and the residue of her estate to her son and daughter. Susanna had not made any lifetime transfers of value.

**How much inheritance tax will be payable on Susanna's estate?**

£

## Task 13

Kendra died in January 2021, aged 93. She has made no lifetime gifts and owned the following assets at death.

Kendra owns the following assets:

(1)   A property valued at £970,000.

(2)   Building society deposits of £387,000.

(3)   Investments in Individual Savings Accounts (ISAs) valued at £39,000 and savings certificates from NS&I (National Savings and Investments) valued at £17,000.

(4)   A life assurance policy on her own life. Proceeds of £225,000 will be received following Kendra's death.

The cost of Kendra's funeral will be £12,800. She also has an outstanding unsecured loan of £1,200 which is due to be repaid on her death.

Under the terms of her will, Kendra has left her entire estate to her nieces and nephews.

The nil rate band of Kendra's husband was 70% utilised when he died ten years ago.

**Calculate the IHT due on Kendra's death.**

(This style of question would be human marked in the exam)

# BPP PRACTICE ASSESSMENT 5
# PERSONAL TAX

## ANSWERS

# Personal Tax (PLTX)
# BPP practice assessment 5

## Task 1

**(a)**

|  | ✓ |
|---|---|
| National Crime Agency | ✓ |
| Association of Taxation Technicians |  |
| Tax Tribunal |  |
| HM Treasury |  |

**(b)**

> **Incorrect tax return**
>
> Inform Jakki of the following:
>
> There may be interest and penalties if there is outstanding tax to pay on the income.
>
> It is an offence not to tell HMRC about this information.
>
> She should tell HMRC as soon as possible and pay any outstanding liabilities.
>
> If she does not want to tell HMRC then her actions could be seen as money laundering.
>
> We would have to cease acting for her and inform HMRC that we have ceased to act.
>
> Do not need to tell HMRC why we have ceased to act due to client confidentiality.

## Task 2

**(a)** **(1)** The cost of the car in the taxable benefit computation is:

£ | 15,200

List price less capital contribution made by Yan.

**(2)** The percentage used in the taxable benefit computation is:

22 | %

14% + (85 − 55)/5% + 2% (pre-April 2020) = 22%

**(3)** The taxable benefit in respect of the provision of fuel for private use is:

| £ | 5,390 |
|---|-------|

£24,500 × 22%

**(b)**

| From: | AATStudent@boxmail.net |
|-------|------------------------|
| **To:** | MTaylor@boxmail.net |
| **Sent:** | 16 June 2021 10:41 |
| **Subject:** | Car |

The provision of the company car will be a taxable benefit because it is available for private use. The benefit is the list price of the car multiplied by a percentage. In this case, because the car has $CO_2$ emissions of between 51 g/km and 54 g/km, the percentage will be 13%. The benefit will therefore be £15,000 × 13% = £1,950 per tax year. There will be no fuel benefit because you will be reimbursing the cost of your private fuel.

There is a statutory mileage allowance which would apply if you use your own car for business purposes. The rate is 45p per mile up to 10,000 miles per year. As your employer would only be paying you 35p per mile, the extra 10p per mile could be claimed by you as an allowable deduction when working out your employment income. If you travelled 6,000 business miles in a tax year, the deduction would be 6,000 × 10p = £600.

## Task 3

**(a)** **(1)** The taxable benefit for 2020/21 is:

| £ | 2,000 |
|---|-------|

£7,000 – £5,000

**(2)**

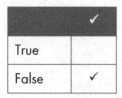

|  | ✓ |
|-------|---|
| True | |
| False | ✓ |

Payments in excess of £6 per week can be exempt benefits provided that evidence can be given that the payment is wholly in respect of additional household expenses incurred by the employee in carrying out their duties at home.

**(b)**

| Item | Wholly or partly taxable | Wholly exempt |
|---|---|---|
| Mobile phone | | ✓ |
| Removal expenses of £9,000 | ✓<br>(limit £8,000) | |
| Incidental personal expenses of working away from home in the UK of £10 per night | ✓<br>(wholly taxable if exceeds £5) | |
| Staff party at cost of £100 per head | | ✓(up to £150) |

**(c)** **(1)** The taxable benefit for 2020/21 is:

£ | 267

Non-cash voucher therefore cost to employer.

If it was a cash voucher the benefit would be face value.

**(2)** The taxable benefit for 2020/21 is:

£ | 158 or 157

£12,000 × (2.25 – 0.5) % × 9/12

# Task 4

**(a)** **(1)** Property income £2,000.

£ | 2,000

**(2)** Premium bond prize £100.

£ | 0

Exempt

**(3)** Government stock interest £80.

£ | 80

**(4)** Dividends received from an ISA of £2,000.

£ | 0

ISA income is exempt

**(b)** **(1)** The amount of the dividend that Marcello will pay income tax on at a rate greater than 0% is:

| £ | 3,400 |
|---|-------|

£5,400 – £2,000 dividend allowance

**(2)** The tax payable on the dividend is:

| £ | 1,295 |
|---|-------|

£3,400 × 38.1%

**(3)**

|       | ✓ |
|-------|---|
| True  |   |
| False | ✓ |

Additional rate taxpayers do not receive a savings allowance.

# Task 5

**(a)** Ronnie's taxable property income for 2020/21 is:

| £ | 5,500 |
|---|-------|

|                              | £     |
|------------------------------|-------|
| Rent accrued £9,000 × 8/12   | 6,000 |
| Less expense £600 × 10/12    | (500) |
| Property income 2020/21      | 5,500 |

**(b)**

|  | 17 Wool Lane £ | 42 Silk Street £ |
|---|---|---|
| Income: |  |  |
| Rents £560/800 × 12 | 6,720 | 9,600 |
| Expenses: |  |  |
| Insurance | (300) | (280) |
| Water rates | (160) | (176) |
| Council tax | (1,800) | (2,100) |
| Cleaning | (800) | (500) |
| New en-suite | 0 | 0 |
| Replacement furniture relief £(3,450 – (700 –150)) | 0 | (2,900) |
| Property income | 3,660 | 3,644 |
| Total property income | 7,304 | |

**(c)** The property income taxable on Asif for 2020/21 is:

| £ | 4,300 |
|---|---|

|  | £ |
|---|---|
| Property 1 profit | 5,000 |
| Property 2 loss | (1,200) |
| Property 3 profit | 2,000 |
|  | 5,800 |
| Less loss b/f | (1,500) |
| Property income 2020/21 | 4,300 |

## Task 6

| | £ |
|---|---|
| Employment income | 58,850 |
| Bank interest | 1,600 |
| Dividends | 9,500 |
| | 69,950 |
| Personal allowance | (12,500) |
| Taxable income | 57,450 |
| **Tax on non-savings income:** | |
| £37,500 × 20% | 7,500 |
| £1,500 (£1,200 × 100/80) × 20% | 300 |
| £7,350 × 40% (£58,850 – £12,500) £46,350 – £37,500 – £1,500) | 2,940 |
| **Tax on savings income:** | |
| £500 × 0% + £1,100 × 40% | 440 |
| **Tax on dividend income:** | |
| £2,000 × 0% + £7,500 × 32½ % | 2,438 |
| Income Tax Liability | 13,618 |

## Task 7

**(a)**

|  | ✓ |
|---|---|
| 1 and 2 |  |
| 1 only | ✓ |
| 2 only |  |
| Neither 1 nor 2 |  |

Suzy is UK resident in the tax year 2020/21 as she is present in the UK for more than half the tax year.

Miles is not UK resident in the tax year 2020/21 as he is not present for more than half the tax year, his only home is not in the UK, and he doesn't work in the UK fulltime.

**(b)**

|  | ✓ |
|---|---|
| 1 and 2 |  |
| 1 and 4 |  |
| 2 and 3 |  |
| 2 and 4 | ✓ |

Interest on an NS&I Investment account and interest on UK Government stocks ('gilts') are taxable.

Premium bond prizes and dividends on shares held in an Individual Savings Account are exempt.

**(c)** **Class 1 Employee**

| £ | 4,380.00 |
|---|---|

**Workings** £(46,000 – 9,500) × 12%

**Class 1 Employer**

| £ | 5,135.26 |
|---|---|

**Workings** £(46,000 – 8,788) × 13.8%

**Class 1A**

| £ | 531.30 |
|---|---|

**Workings** £3,850 × 13.8%

## Task 8

**(a)** The salary to be included in employment income for 2020/21 is:

£ | 36,180

| | £ |
|---|---|
| Salary April to December 2020: 9/12 × £36,000 | 27,000 |
| Salary January to March 2021: 3/12 × £(36,000 × 102%) | 9,180 |

**(b)** The bonus to be included in employment income for 2020/21 is:

£ | 2,000

Bonus received 31 March 2021

**(c)** The commission to be included in employment income for 2020/21 is:

£ | 0

Commission received 30 April 2021 (taxable in 2021/22)

**(d)** The benefit to be included in employment income for 2020/21 is:

£ | 0

Exempt benefit

········································································································

## Task 9

**(a)**

| Asset | Chargeable | Exempt |
|---|---|---|
| Horse | | ✓ (wasting asset) |
| Field in which horse is kept | ✓ | |
| Antique horse brass costing £500, worth £1,700 | | ✓ (exempt chattel - cost and proceeds < £6,000) |

**(b)** The chargeable gain on sale is:

£ | 45,000

| | £ |
|---|---|
| Proceeds of sale | 125,000 |
| Less cost | (65,000) |
| enhancement expenditure | (15,000) |
| Chargeable gain | 45,000 |

Redecoration is a revenue expense, not capital, and therefore not allowable.

**(c)** The allowable loss on sale is:

£ | 2,300

| | £ |
|---|---|
| Deemed disposal proceeds | 6,000 |
| Less disposal costs £(2,700 × 100/90) × 10% | (300) |
| Net proceeds | 5,700 |
| Less cost | (8,000) |
| Allowable loss | (2,300) |

**(d)** The chargeable gain on sale is:

£ | 107,500

| | £ |
|---|---|
| Proceeds | 125,000 |
| Less: part disposal<br>£70,000 × (125,000/(125,000 + 375,000)) | (17,500) |
| Chargeable gain | 107,500 |

## Task 10

**Gain**

|  | £ |
|---|---|
| Proceeds of sale | 8,000 |
| Less cost | (4,560) |
| Chargeable gain | 3,440 |

**Share pool**

|  | No of shares | Cost £ |
|---|---|---|
| August 2009 Acquisition | 2,000 | 5,000 |
| September 2012 Bonus issue 1 for 1 | 2,000 | 0 |
| October 2014 Acquisition | 1,000 | 7,000 |
|  | 5,000 | 12,000 |
| November 2016 Rights issue 3 for 2 | 7,500 | 45,000 |
|  | 12,500 | 57,000 |
| June 2020 Disposal (1,000/12,500 × £57,000) | (1,000) | (4,560) |
| c/f | 11,500 | 52,440 |

........................................................................

## Task 11

**(a)** The CGT payable for 2020/21 is:

£ | 629

|  | £ |
|---|---|
| Gains | 17,000 |
| Less annual exempt amount | (12,300) |
| Less loss b/f | (1,000) |
| Taxable gains | 3,700 |
| CGT |  |

|  | £ |
|---|---|
| £1,110 (W) × 10% | 111 |
| £2,590 × 20% | 518 |
| CGT | 629 |

(W) Unused basic rate band is £37,500 + £500 (£400 × 100/80) − £36,890 = £1,110

**(b)**

|  | ✓ |
|---|---|
| True |  |
| False | ✓ |

Provided the house has been occupied by the owner as his only or main residence at some time during the period of ownership, the last nine months of ownership are exempt whether or not the owner lives in the house during that period.

# Task 12

**(a)**

|  | ✓ |
|---|---|
| £0 |  |
| £31,250 |  |
| £29,750 | ✓ |
| £23,800 |  |

**Workings**

|  | £ |
|---|---|
| Gift | 190,000 |
| Less AE × 2 (20/21 + 19/20 b/f) | (6,000) |
|  | 184,000 |
| Less nil rate band available (£325,000 – 260,000) | (65,000) |
|  | 119,000 |
| IHT @ 20/80 | £29,750 |

The answer £0 does not restrict the nil rate band. The answer £31,250 does not deduct the annual exemptions. The answer £23,800 calculates tax at 20%.

**(b)**

| | ✓ |
|---|---|
| £84,000 | |
| £27,000 | |
| £66,000 | ✓ |
| £45,000 | |

**Workings**

| | £ |
|---|---|
| Before the gift: 100% shareholding 1,000 × £150 | 150,000 |
| After the gift: 70% shareholding 700 × £120 | (84,000) |
| Transfer of value | 66,000 |

The answer £84,000 is the value of Dan's shareholding after the gift. The answer £27,000 is the value of a 30% shareholding. The answer £45,000 is 300 shares at £150 value per share.

**(c)**

| £ | 14,000 |
|---|---|

| | £ |
|---|---|
| House (net of mortgage) £(245,000 – 60,000) | 185,000 |
| Investments and cash | 455,000 |
| | 640,000 |
| Less funeral expenses | (5,000) |
| | 635,000 |
| Less exempt gift to spouse | (100,000) |
| Chargeable death estate | 535,000 |

| | |
|---|---|
| Less residence nil rate band (home left to direct descendants) | (175,000) |
| Less available nil rate band (no lifetime transfers) | (325,000) |
| | 35,000 |
| IHT @ 40% | 14,000 |

## Task 13

| | £ |
|---|---|
| Property | 970,000 |
| Building society deposits | 387,000 |
| Individual Savings Accounts | 39,000 |
| NS&I certificates | 17,000 |
| Proceeds of life policy | 225,000 |
| Gross estate | 1,638,000 |
| Less funeral expenses | (12,800) |
| loan | (1,200) |
| Net estate | 1,624,000 |
| **Inheritance tax** | |
| £325,000 + (£325,000 × 30%) @ 0% | 0 |
| £1,201,500 @ 40% | 480,600 |
| Inheritance tax liability | 480,600 |

No RNRB is available as the property was not left to direct descendants.

## Tax tables 2020/21

# 1 Tax rates and bands

| Tax rates | Tax bands | Normal rates % | Dividend rates % |
|---|---|---|---|
| Basic rate | £1–£37,500 | 20 | 7.5 |
| Higher rate | £37,501–£150,000 | 40 | 32.5 |
| Additional rate | £150,001 and over | 45 | 38.1 |

# 2 Allowances

| | | £ |
|---|---|---|
| Personal allowance | | 12,500 |
| Savings allowance: | Basic rate taxpayer | 1,000 |
| | Higher rate taxpayer | 500 |
| Dividend allowance | | 2,000 |
| Income limit for personal allowances* | | 100,000 |

* Personal allowances are reduced by £1 for every £2 over the income limit.

# 3 Property income allowance

| | £ |
|---|---|
| Annual limit | 1,000 |

# 4 Individual savings accounts

| | £ |
|---|---|
| Annual limit | 20,000 |

# 5 Car benefit percentage

| $CO_2$ Emissions for petrol engines g/km | Electric range miles | Cars first registered from 6 April 2020 % |
|---|---|---|
| Nil | | 0 |
| 1 to 50 | 130 or more | 0 |
| 1 to 50 | 70-129 | 3 |
| 1 to 50 | 40-69 | 6 |
| 1 to 50 | 30-39 | 10 |
| 1 to 50 | Less than 30 | 12 |
| 51 to 54 | | 13 |
| 55 or more | | 14 + 1% for every extra 5g/km above 55g/km |
| Registration pre 6 April 2020* | | Additional 2% |
| Diesel engines** | | Additional 4% |

\* The additional 2% does not apply to pure electric vehicles

\*\* The additional 4% will not apply to diesel cars which are registered after 1 September 2017 and they meet the RDE2 standards.

# 6 Car fuel benefit

|  | £ |
|---|---|
| Base figure | 24,500 |

# 7 Approved mileage allowance payments (employees and residential landlords)

| | |
|---|---|
| First 10,000 miles | 45p per mile |
| Over 10,000 miles | 25p per mile |
| Additional passengers | 5p per mile per passenger |
| Motorcycles | 24p per mile |
| Bicycles | 20p per mile |

# 8 Van benefit charge

|  | £ |
|---|---|
| Basic charge | 3,490 |
| Private fuel charge | 666 |
|  | % |
| Benefit charge for zero emission vans | 80 |

# 9 Other benefits in kind

| | |
|---|---|
| Expensive accommodation limit | £75,000 |
| Health screening | One per year |
| Incidental overnight expenses: within UK | £5 per night |
| Incidental overnight expenses: overseas | £10 per night |
| Job-related accommodation | £Nil |
| Living expenses where job-related exemption applies | Restricted to 10% of employees net earnings |
| Loan of assets annual charge | 20% |
| Low-rate or interest free loans | Up to £10,000 |
| Mobile telephones | One per employee |
| Non-cash gifts from someone other than the employer | £250 per tax year |
| Non-cash long service award | £50 per year of service |

| | |
|---|---|
| Pay whilst attending a full time course | £15,480 per academic year |
| Provision of eye tests and spectacles for VDU use | £Nil |
| Provision of parking spaces | £Nil |
| Provision of workplace childcare | £Nil |
| Provision of workplace sports facilities | £Nil |
| Removal and relocation expenses | £8,000 |
| Staff party or event | £150 per head |
| Staff suggestion scheme | Up to £5,000 |
| Subsidised meals | £Nil |
| Working from home | £6 per week / £26 per month |

## 10 HMRC official rate

| | |
|---|---|
| HMRC official rate | 2.25% |

## 11 National insurance contributions

| | | % |
|---|---|---|
| Class 1 Employee: | Below £9,500 | 0 |
| | Above £9,500 and Below £50,000 | 12 |
| | £50,000 and above | 2 |
| Class 1 Employer: | Below £8,788 | 0 |
| | £8,788 and above | 13.8 |
| Class 1A | | 13.8 |
| | | £ |
| Employment allowance | | 4,000 |

## 12 Capital gains tax

| | £ |
|---|---|
| Annual exempt amount | 12,300 |

## 13 Capital gains tax - tax rates

| | % |
|---|---|
| Basic rate | 10 |
| Higher rate | 20 |

# 14 Inheritance tax – tax rates

|  |  | £ |
|---|---|---|
| Nil rate band |  | 325,000 |
| Additional residence nil-rate band* |  | 175,000 |
|  |  | % |
| Excess taxable at: | Death rate | 40 |
|  | Lifetime rate | 20 |

* Applies when a home is passed on death to direct descendants of the deceased after 6 April 2017. Any unused band is transferrable to a spouse or civil partner.

# 15 Inheritance tax – tapering relief

|  | % reduction |
|---|---|
| 3 years or less | 0 |
| Over 3 years but less than 4 years | 20 |
| Over 4 years but less than 5 years | 40 |
| Over 5 years but less than 6 years | 60 |
| Over 6 years but less than 7 years | 80 |

# 16 Inheritance – exemptions

|  |  | £ |
|---|---|---|
| Small gifts |  | 250 per transferee per tax year |
| Marriage or civil partnership: | From parent | 5,000 |
|  | Grandparent | 2,500 |
|  | One party to the other | 2,500 |
|  | Others | 1,000 |
| Annual exemption |  | 3,000 |

# 17 Deemed domicile

| Deemed domicile | Criteria |
|---|---|
| Condition A | Was born in the UK |
|  | Domicile of origin was in the UK |
|  | Was resident in the UK for 2017 to 2018 or later years |
| Condition B | Has been UK resident for at least 15 of the 20 tax years immediately before the relevant tax year |

## Reference material

# 1 Interpretation and abbreviations

### Context

Tax advisors operate in a complex business and financial environment. The increasing public focus on the role of taxation in wider society means a greater interest in the actions of tax advisors and their clients.

This guidance, written by the professional bodies for their members working in tax, sets out the hallmarks of a good tax advisor, and in particular the fundamental principles of behaviour that members are expected to follow.

### Interpretation

1.1    In this guidance:

- 'Client' includes, where the context requires, 'former client'.

- 'Member' (and 'members') includes 'firm' or 'practice' and the staff thereof.

- Words in the singular include the plural and words in the plural include the singular.

### Abbreviations

1.2    The following abbreviations have been used:

| AML | Anti-Money Laundering |
|---|---|
| CCAB | Consultative Committee of Accountancy Bodies |
| DOTAS | Disclosure of Tax Avoidance Schemes |
| GAAP | Generally Accepted Accounting Principles |
| GAAR | General Anti-Abuse Rule in Finance Act 2013 |
| GDPR | General Data Protection Regulation |
| HMRC | Her Majesty's Revenue and Customs |
| MTD | Making Tax Digital |
| MLRO | Money Laundering Reporting Officer |
| NCA | National Crime Agency (previously the Serious Organised Crime Agency, SOCA) |

| POTAS | Promoters of Tax Avoidance Schemes |
|-------|-------------------------------------|
| PCRT | Professional Conduct in Relation to Taxation |
| SRN | Scheme Reference Number |

# 2 Fundamental principles

## Overview of the fundamental principles

2.1 Ethical behaviour in the tax profession is critical. The work carried out by a member needs to be trusted by society at large as well as by clients and other stakeholders. What a member does reflects not just on themselves but on the profession as a whole.

2.2 A member must comply with the following fundamental principles:

### Integrity

To be straightforward and honest in all professional and business relationships.

### Objectivity

To not allow bias, conflict of interest or undue influence of others to override professional or business judgements.

### Professional competence and due care

To maintain professional knowledge and skill at the level required to ensure that a client or employer receives competent professional service based on current developments in practice, legislation and techniques and act diligently and in accordance with applicable technical and professional standards.

### Confidentiality

To respect the confidentiality of information acquired as a result of professional and business relationships and, therefore, not disclose any such information to third parties without proper and specific authority, unless there is a legal or professional right or duty to disclose, nor use the information for the personal advantage of the member or third parties.

### Professional behaviour

To comply with relevant laws and regulations and avoid any action that discredits the profession.

# 3 PCRT Help sheet A: Submission of tax information and 'Tax filings'

### Definition of filing of tax information and tax filings (filing)

3.1 For the purposes of this guidance, the term 'filing' includes any online submission of data, online filing or other filing that is prepared on behalf of the client for the purposes of disclosing to any taxing authority details that are to be used in the calculation of tax due by a client or a refund of tax due to the client or for other official purposes. It includes all taxes, NIC and duties.

3.2 A letter, or online notification, giving details in respect of a filing or as an amendment to a filing including, for example, any voluntary disclosure of an error should be dealt with as if it was a filing.

### Making Tax Digital and filing

3.3 Tax administration systems, including the UK's, are increasingly moving to mandatory digital filing of tax information and returns.

3.4 Except in exceptional circumstances, a member will explicitly file in their capacity as agent. A member is advised to use the facilities provided for agents and to avoid knowing or using the client's personal access credentials.

3.5 A member should keep their access credentials safe from unauthorised use and consider periodic change of passwords.

3.6 A member is recommended to forward suspicious emails to phishing@hmrc.gsi.gov.uk and then delete them. It is also important to avoid clicking on websites or links in suspicious emails, or opening attachments.

3.7 Firms should have policies on cyber security, AML and GDPR.

### Taxpayer's responsibility

3.8 The taxpayer has primary responsibility to submit correct and complete filings to the best of their knowledge and belief. The final decision as to whether to disclose any issue is that of the client but in relation to your responsibilities see paragraph 12 below.

3.9 In annual self-assessment returns or returns with short filing periods the filing may include reasonable estimates where necessary.

### Member's responsibility

3.10 A member who prepares a filing on behalf of a client is responsible to the client for the accuracy of the filing based on the information provided.

3.11 In dealing with HMRC in relation to a client's tax affairs a member should bear in mind their duty of confidentiality to the client and that they are acting as the agent of their client. They have a duty to act in the best interests of their client.

3.12 A member should act in good faith in dealings with HMRC in accordance with the fundamental principle of integrity. In particular the member should take reasonable care and exercise appropriate professional scepticism when making statements or asserting facts on behalf of a client.

3.13 Where acting as a tax agent, a member is not required to audit the figures in the books and records provided or verify information provided by a client or by a third party. However, a member should take care not to be associated with the presentation of facts they know or believe to be incorrect or misleading, not to assert tax positions in a tax filing which they consider to have no sustainable basis.

3.14 When a member is communicating with HMRC, they should consider whether they need to make it clear to what extent they are relying on information which has been supplied by the client or a third party.

## Materiality

3.15 Whether an amount is to be regarded as material depends upon the facts and circumstances of each case.

3.16 The profits of a trade, profession, vocation or property business should be computed in accordance with GAAP subject to any adjustment required or authorised by law in computing profits for those purposes. This permits a trade, profession, vocation or property business to disregard non-material adjustments in computing its accounting profits.

3.17 The application of GAAP, and therefore materiality does not extend beyond the accounting profits. Thus, the accounting concept of materiality cannot be applied when completing tax filings.

3.18 It should be noted that for certain small businesses an election may be made to use the cash basis instead; for small property businesses the default position is the cash basis. Where the cash basis is used, materiality is not relevant.

## Disclosure

3.19 If a client is unwilling to include in a tax filing the minimum information required by law, the member should follow the guidance in Help sheet C: Dealing with Errors. The paragraphs below (paras 20 – 24) give guidance on some of the more common areas of uncertainty over disclosure.

3.20 In general, it is likely to be in a client's own interests to ensure that factors relevant to their tax liability are adequately disclosed to HMRC because:

- their relationship with HMRC is more likely to be on a satisfactory footing if they can demonstrate good faith in their dealings with them.

HMRC notes in 'Your Charter' that 'We want to give you a service that is fair, accurate and based on mutual trust and respect'

- they will reduce the risk of a discovery or further assessment and may reduce exposure to interest and penalties.

3.21 It may be advisable to consider fuller disclosure than is strictly necessary. Reference to 'The Standards for Tax Planning' in PCRT may be relevant. The factors involved in making this decision include:

- a filing relies on a valuation
- the terms of the applicable law
- the view taken by the member
- the extent of any doubt that exists
- the manner in which disclosure is to be made
- the size and gravity of the item in question.

3.22 When advocating fuller disclosure than is necessary a member should ensure that their client is adequately aware of the issues involved and their potential implications. Fuller disclosure should only be made with the client's consent.

3.23 Cases will arise where there is doubt as to the correct treatment of an item of income or expenditure, or the computation of a gain or allowance. In such cases a member ought to consider what additional disclosure, if any, might be necessary. For example, additional disclosure should be considered where:

- there is inherent doubt as to the correct treatment of an item, for example, expenditure on repairs which might be regarded as capital in whole or part, or the VAT liability of a particular transaction, or

- HMRC has published its interpretation or has indicated its practice on a point, but the client proposes to adopt a different view, whether or not supported by Counsel's opinion. The member should refer to the guidance on the Veltema case and the paragraph below. See also HMRC guidance.

3.24 A member who is uncertain whether their client should disclose a particular item or of its treatment should consider taking further advice before reaching a decision. They should use their best endeavours to ensure that the client understands the issues, implications and the proposed course of action. Such a decision may have to be justified at a later date, so the member's files should contain sufficient evidence to support the position taken, including timely notes of discussions with the client and/or with other advisors, copies of any second opinion obtained and the client's final decision. A failure to take reasonable care may result in HMRC imposing a penalty if an error is identified after an enquiry.

## Supporting documents

3.25 For the most part, HMRC does not consider that it is necessary for a taxpayer to provide supporting documentation in order to satisfy the taxpayer's overriding need to make a correct filing. HMRC's view is that, where it is necessary for that purpose, explanatory information should be entered in the 'white space' provided on the filing. However, HMRC does recognise that the taxpayer may wish to supply further details of a particular computation or transaction in order to minimise the risk of a discovery assessment being raised at a later time. Following the uncertainty created by the decision in Veltema, HMRC's guidance can be found in SP1/06 – Self Assessment: Finality and Discovery.

3.26 Further HMRC guidance says that sending attachments with a tax filing is intended for those cases where the taxpayer 'feels it is crucial to provide additional information to support the filing but for some reason cannot utilise the white space'.

## Reliance on HMRC published guidance

3.27 Whilst it is reasonable in most circumstances to rely on HMRC published guidance, a member should be aware that the Tribunal and the courts will apply the law even if this conflicts with HMRC guidance.

3.28 Notwithstanding this, if a client has relied on HMRC guidance which is clear and unequivocal and HMRC resiles from any of the terms of the guidance, a Judicial Review claim is a possible route to pursue.

## Approval of tax filings

3.29 The member should advise the client to review their tax filing before it is submitted.

3.30 The member should draw the client's attention to the responsibility which the client is taking in approving the filing as correct and complete. Attention should be drawn to any judgmental areas or positions reflected in the filing to ensure that the client is aware of these and their implications before they approve the filing.

3.31 A member should obtain evidence of the client's approval of the filing in electronic or non-electronic form.

# 4 PCRT Help sheet B: Tax advice

## The Standards for Tax Planning

4.1 The Standards for Tax Planning are critical to any planning undertaken by members. They are:

- Client Specific

  Tax planning must be specific to the particular client's facts and circumstances. Clients must be alerted to the wider risks and implications of any courses of action.

- Lawful

  At all times members must act lawfully and with integrity and expect the same from their clients. Tax planning should be based on a realistic assessment of the facts and on a credible view of the law.

  Members should draw their client's attention to where the law is materially uncertain, for example because HMRC is known to take a different view of the law. Members should consider taking further advice appropriate to the risks and circumstances of the particular case, for example where litigation is likely.

- Disclosure and transparency

  Tax advice must not rely for its effectiveness on HMRC having less than the relevant facts. Any disclosure must fairly represent all relevant facts.

- Tax planning arrangements

  Members must not create, encourage or promote tax planning arrangements or structures that i) set out to achieve results that are contrary to the clear intention of Parliament in enacting relevant legislation and/or ii) are highly artificial or highly contrived and seek to exploit shortcomings within the relevant legislation.

- Professional judgement and appropriate documentation

- Applying these requirements to particular client advisory situations requires members to exercise professional judgement on a number of matters. Members should keep notes on a timely basis of the rationale for the judgements exercised in seeking to adhere to these requirements

## Guidance

4.2 The paragraphs below provide guidance for members when considering whether advice complies with the Fundamental Principles and Standards for Tax Planning.

### Tax evasion

4.3 A member should never be knowingly involved in tax evasion, although, of course, it is appropriate to act for a client who is rectifying their affairs.

### Tax planning and advice

4.4 In contrast to tax evasion, tax planning is legal. However, under the Standard members 'must not create, encourage or promote tax planning arrangements that (i) set out to achieve results that are contrary to the clear intention of Parliament in enacting relevant legislation and/or (ii) are highly artificial or highly contrived and seek to exploit shortcomings within the relevant legislation'.

4.5 Things to consider:

- Have you checked that your engagement letter fully covers the scope of the planning advice?

- Have you taken the Standards for Tax Planning and the Fundamental Principles into account? Is it client specific? Is it lawful? Will all relevant facts be disclosed to HMRC? Is it creating, encouraging or promoting tax planning contrary to the 4th Standard for Tax Planning.

- How tax sophisticated is the client?

- Has the client made clear what they wish to achieve by the planning?

- What are the issues involved with the implementation of the planning?

- What are the risks associated with the planning and have you warned the client of the them? For example:

    - The strength of the legal interpretation relied upon.

    - The potential application of the GAAR.

    - The implications for the client, including the obligations of the client in relation to their tax return, if the planning requires disclosure under DOTAS or DASVOIT and the potential for an accelerated payment notice or partner payment notice?

    - The reputational risk to the client and the member of the planning in the public arena.

    - The stress, cost and wider personal or business implications to the client in the event of a prolonged dispute with HMRC. This may involve unwelcomed publicity, costs, expenses and loss of management time over a significant period.

    - If the client tenders for government contracts, the potential impact of the proposed tax planning on tendering for and retaining public sector contracts.

- The risk of counteraction. This may occur before the planning is completed or potentially there may be retrospective counteraction at a later date.

- The risk of challenge by HMRC. Such challenge may relate to the legal interpretation relied upon, but may alternatively relate to the construction of the facts, including the implementation of the planning.

- The risk and inherent uncertainty of litigation. The probability of the planning being overturned by the courts if litigated and the potential ultimate downside should the client be unsuccessful.

- Is a second opinion necessary/advisable?

- Are the arrangements in line with any applicable code of conduct or ethical guidelines or stances for example the Banking Code, and fit and proper tests for charity trustees and pension administrators?

- Are you satisfied that the client understands the planning proposed?

- Have you documented the advice given and the reasoning behind it?

# 5 PCRT Help sheet C: Dealing with errors

## Introduction

5.1 For the purposes of this guidance, the term 'error' is intended to include all errors and mistakes whether they were made by the client, the member, HMRC or any other party involved in a client's tax affairs, and whether made innocently or deliberately.

5.2 During a member's relationship with the client, the member may become aware of possible errors in the client's tax affairs. Unless the client is already aware of the possible error, they should be informed as soon as the member identifies them.

5.3 Where the error has resulted in the client paying too much tax the member should advise the client to make a repayment claim. The member should advise the client of the time limits to make a claim and have regard to any relevant time limits. The rest of this Help sheet deals with situations where tax may be due to HMRC.

5.4 Sometimes an error made by HMRC may mean that the client has not paid tax actually due or they have been incorrectly repaid tax. There may be fee costs as a result of correcting such mistakes. A member should bear in mind that, in some circumstances, clients or agents may be able to claim for additional professional costs incurred and compensation from HMRC.

5.5 A member should act correctly from the outset. A member should keep sufficient appropriate records of discussions and advice and when dealing with errors the member should:

- give the client appropriate advice';

- if necessary, so long as they continue to act for the client, seek to persuade the client to behave correctly;

- take care not to appear to be assisting a client to plan or commit any criminal offence or to conceal any offence which has been committed; and

- in appropriate situations, or where in doubt, discuss the client's situation with a colleague or an independent third party (having due regard to client confidentiality).

5.6 Once aware of a possible error, a member must bear in mind the legislation on money laundering and the obligations and duties which this places upon them.

5.7 Where the member may have made the error, the member should consider whether they need to notify their professional indemnity insurers.

5.8 In any situation where a member has concerns about their own position, they should consider taking specialist legal advice. For example, where a client appears to have used the member to assist in the commissioning of a criminal offence and people could question whether the member had acted honestly in in good faith. Note that The Criminal Finances Act 2017 has created new criminal offences of failure to prevent facilitation of tax evasion.

5.9 The flowchart below summarises the recommended steps a member should take where a possible error arises. It must be read in conjunction with the guidance and commentary that follow it.

311

# Dealing with errors flowchart

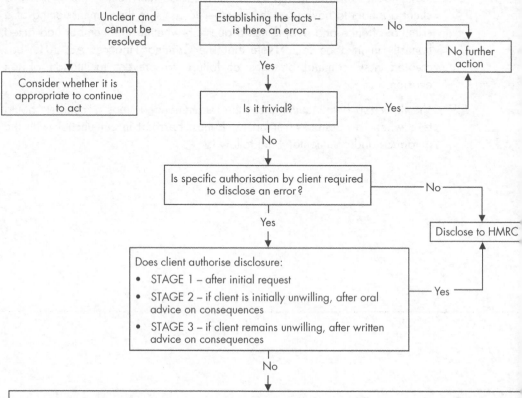

**YOU MUST CEASE TO ACT**

- Advise client in writing that you no longer act for them in respect of any tax matters and, if relevant, any other client matters.
- Notify HMRC that you have ceased to act, if relevant.
- Consider if you need to advise HMRC that any accounts/statements carrying a report signed by you can no longer be relied upon.
- Consider whether a report should be made to MLRO/NCA.
- Carefully consider your response to any professional enquiry letter.

At all times consider your obligations under anti-money laundering legislation and whether you need to submit a Suspicious Activity Report.

# 6 PCRT Help sheet D: Requests for data by HMRC

## Introduction

6.1 For the purposes of this help sheet the term 'data' includes documents in whatever form (including electronic) and other information. While this guidance relates to HMRC requests, other government bodies or organisations may also approach the member for data. The same principles apply.

6.2 A distinction should be drawn between a request for data made informally ('informal requests') and those requests for data which are made in exercise of a power to require the provision of the data requested ('formal requests').

6.3 Similarly, requests addressed to a client and those addressed to a member require different handling.

6.4 Where a member no longer acts for a client, the member remains subject to the duty of confidentiality. In relation to informal requests, the member should refer the enquirer either to the former client or if authorised by the client to the new agent. In relation to formal requests addressed to the member, the termination of their professional relationship with the client does not affect the member's duty to comply with that request, where legally required to do so.

6.5 A member should comply with formal requests and should not seek to frustrate legitimate requests for information. Adopting a constructive approach may help to resolve issues promptly and minimise costs to all parties.

6.6 Whilst a member should be aware of HMRC's powers it may be appropriate to take specialist advice.

6.7 Devolved tax authorities have separate powers.

6.8 Two flowcharts are at the end of this help sheet;

- Requests for data addressed to the member, and
- Requests for data addressed to the client.

## Informal requests addressed to the client

6.9 From time to time HMRC chooses to communicate directly with clients rather than with the appointed agent.

6.10 HMRC has given reassurances that it is working to ensure that initial contact on compliance checks will normally be via the agent and only if the agent does not reply within an appropriate timescale will the contact be directly with the client.

6.11 When the member assists a client in dealing with such requests from HMRC, the member should advise the client that cooperation with informal requests can provide greater opportunities for the taxpayer to find a pragmatic way to work through the issue at hand with HMRC.

## Informal requests addressed to the member

6.12 Disclosure in response to informal requests can only be made with the client's permission.

6.13 In many instances, the client will have authorised routine disclosure of relevant data, for example, through the engagement letter. However, if there is any doubt about whether the client has authorised disclosure, the member should ask the client to approve what is to be disclosed.

6.14 Where an oral enquiry is made by HMRC, a member should consider asking for it to be put in writing so that a response may be agreed with the client.

6.15 Although there is no obligation to comply with an informal request in whole or in part, a member should advise the client whether it is in the client's best interests to disclose such data, as lack of cooperation may have a direct impact on penalty negotiations post—enquiry.

6.16 Informal requests may be forerunners to formal requests compelling the disclosure of data. Consequently, it may be sensible to comply with such requests.

## Formal requests addressed to the client

6.17 In advising their client a member should consider whether specialist advice may be needed, for example on such issues as whether the notice has been issued in accordance with the relevant tax legislation and whether the data request is valid.

6.18 The member should also advise the client about any relevant right of appeal against the formal request if appropriate and of the consequences of a failure to comply.

6.19 If the notice is legally effective the client is legally obliged to comply with the request.

6.20 The most common statutory notice issued to clients and third parties by HMRC is under Schedule 36 FA 2008.

## Formal requests addressed to the member

6.21 The same principles apply to formal requests to the member as formal requests to clients.

6.22 If a formal request is valid it **overrides the member's duty of confidentiality** to their client. The member is therefore obliged to comply with the request. Failure to comply with their legal obligations can expose the member to civil or criminal penalties.

6.23 In cases where the member is not legally precluded by the terms of the notice from communicating with the client, the member should advise the client of the notice and keep the client informed of progress and developments.

6.24 The member should ensure that in complying with any notice they do not provide information or data outside the scope of the notice.

6.25 If a member is faced with a situation in which HMRC is seeking to enforce disclosure by the removal of data, or seeking entrance to inspect business premises occupied by a member in their capacity as an adviser, the member should consider seeking immediate professional advice, to ensure that this is the legally correct course of action.

## Privileged data

6.26 Legal privilege arises under common law and may only be overridden if this is set out in legislation. It protects a party's right to communicate in confidence with a legal adviser. The privilege belongs to the client and not to the member.

6.27 If a document is privileged: The client cannot be required to make disclosure of that document to HMRC. Another party cannot disclose it (including the member), without the client's express permission.

6.28 There are two types of legal privilege under common law: legal advice privilege and litigation privilege.

(a) **Legal advice privilege**

Covers documents passing between a client and their legal adviser prepared for the purposes of obtaining or giving legal advice. However, communications from a tax adviser who is not a practising lawyer will not attract legal advice privilege even if such individuals are giving advice on legal matters such as tax law.

(b) **Litigation privilege**

Covers data created for the dominant purpose of litigation. Litigation privilege may arise where litigation has not begun, but is merely contemplated and may apply to data prepared by non-lawyer advisors (including tax advisors). There are two important limits on litigation privilege. First, it does not arise in respect of non-adversarial proceedings. Second, the documents must be produced for the 'dominant purpose' of litigation.

6.29 A privilege under Schedule 36 paragraphs 19, (documents relating to the conduct of a pending appeal), 24 and 25 (auditors, and tax advisors' documents) might exist by "quasi-privilege" and if this is the case a tax adviser does not have to provide those documents. Care should be taken as not all data may be privileged.

6.30 A member who receives a request for data, some of which the member believes may be subject to privilege or 'quasi-privilege', should take independent legal advice on the position, unless expert in this area.

## Helpsheet D: Flowchart regarding requests for data by HMRC to the Member

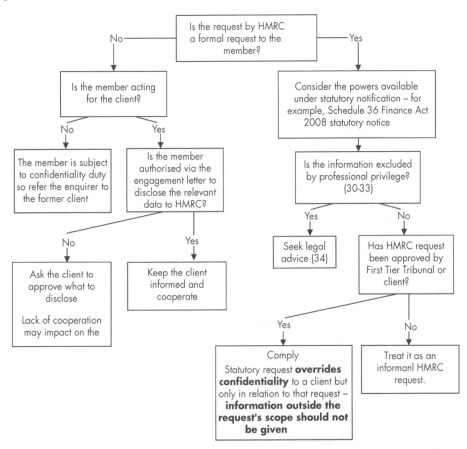

## Helpsheet D: Flowchart regarding requests for data by HMRC to the Client

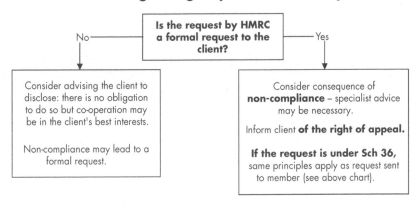

The Reference Materials have been produced by the AAT.

1P07-16821-012